Design, Launch, and Scale IoT Services

A Practical Business Approach

Barry Haughian

Apress®

Design, Launch, and Scale IoT Services: A Practical Business Approach

Barry Haughian
Galway, Ireland

ISBN-13 (pbk): 978-1-4842-3711-3   ISBN-13 (electronic): 978-1-4842-3712-0
https://doi.org/10.1007/978-1-4842-3712-0

Library of Congress Control Number: 2018955491

Managing Director, Apress Media LLC: Welmoed Spahr
Acquisitions Editor: Natalie Pao
Development Editor: James Markham
Coordinating Editor: Jessica Vakili

Cover designed by eStudioCalamar

Cover image designed by Freepik (www.freepik.com)

Distributed to the book trade worldwide by Springer Science+Business Media New York, 233 Spring Street, 6th Floor, New York, NY 10013. Phone 1-800-SPRINGER, fax (201) 348-4505, e-mail orders-ny@springer-sbm.com, or visit www.springeronline.com. Apress Media, LLC is a California LLC and the sole member (owner) is Springer Science + Business Media Finance Inc (SSBM Finance Inc). SSBM Finance Inc is a **Delaware** corporation.

For information on translations, please e-mail rights@apress.com, or visit www.apress.com/rights-permissions.

Apress titles may be purchased in bulk for academic, corporate, or promotional use. eBook versions and licenses are also available for most titles. For more information, reference our Print and eBook Bulk Sales web page at www.apress.com/bulk-sales.

Any source code or other supplementary material referenced by the author in this book is available to readers on GitHub via the book's product page, located at www.apress.com/978-1-4842-3711-3. For more detailed information, please visit www.apress.com/source-code.

Printed on acid-free paper

Table of Contents

About the Author

Barry Haughian is a graduate of Aberdeen University, MSC Artificial Intelligence and Queens University Belfast, BSC Computer Science. He has been working in IT for 20+ years providing IT and Telecommunication consultancy services to a broad range of companies. During the last 10 years he has developed services in multiple IoT industry verticals, including Industry 4.0, Smart Transport, Smart Energy, Smart City, and Connected Home. He has worked with all aspects of IoT services including the development of GTM strategies, Commercial, Operational and Technical models developed in collaboration with Fortune 500 companies, IoT startups, service partners, and competitors.

Acknowledgments

When I embarked on my IoT journey, I had already worked with machine-to-machine (M2M) connectivity services for several years. I was requested to initiate an IoT innovation program to develop IoT cloud service offerings for Ericsson. Many sponsors expected that we would create an IoT platform to facilitate the launching of IoT services, but I set our targets a little higher. I wanted to wrap the IoT products we were planning to develop in the as-a-service (AaS) business model, bringing stakeholders, collaborators, and customers on an "IoT journey." To quote the Head of XaaS at Ericsson, "The innovation will not be technology; it will be development of a new business model and delivery method for IoT services at Ericsson."

In 2015, Ericsson hosted an IoT conference in Stockholm where the keynote speaker suggested, "If you haven't started in the IoT, you are already late. If you have started, then you will need to launch your offering immediately." I believed that then but don't believe it now. IoT will be around for a long time; there will be new IoT services, ideas, and business models with revenue streams continuously launched. You will never be too late with new, innovative ideas, and IoT offers increased possibilities for realizing your vision.

Fast-forward two years, and the IoT Accelerator is launched at Messe Hannover, the international industrial trade fair.

During this period, there have been hundreds of contributors across the globe from the Ericsson organization working in areas such as sales, commercial management, delivery and operations, and research and development. The engagements with partners, collaborators, clients, and even competitors have provided a great learning experience for the team as we all continue with our IoT journey.

ACKNOWLEDGMENTS

This book summarizes many of these discussions, the mistakes, the successes, and the subsequent conclusions. There have been many collaborators who have added their unique expertise to enable this book to be completed. I would like to thank Grant Smith, Head of Smart Energy in Queensland, Australia, who helped to initiate many of the innovative IoT discussions. There were over more than 150 direct contributors during the development of the IoT concepts outlined in the book, the senior managers were Paul McGettrick, Marina Acedo and Gema LaFuente, Jason Chua and Maria Archer. Technical support during the editing process was provided by Luiz (Tayo) Carvahal, Principal Solution Architect at Microsoft and Paula Kelly, Lecturer at D.I.T. Grant Marshall VP Supply Network Head of Engineering at Nokia, Mikael Blockstrand Head of M2M Ericsson and Luis (Tayo) Carvahal provided great insights into the future of IoT. Thanks also to Marina Acedo, Senior Project Manager at Avya, Andrew Parker Operations Manager at Ericsson and Andres Amores, Head of IoT Smart Services for their input on Operational topics. Finally, I would like to thank Mikael Ungerholm, Head of Innovation at Ericsson Tony Sandberg, Innovation Consultant and Ericsson, Paolo Filetti, Head of Digital Solutions at Bridgestone, Henrik Bergman Head of Sales MTEK and Peter Lejon CEO virtuGrp for providing support during this IoT journey.

Preface

The Internet has given unlimited access to data and technology for most of the world's population. We have all become very tech savvy. The Internet of Things revolution promises to bring this to the next level with the volumes of services, devices and humans communicating growing exponentially over the next few decades.

There are many factors contributing to the IoT revolution. Mobile device communication services allow devices and humans to be permanently connected. Cloud services have reduced the complexity required to produce new services and products. The advances in device design and manufacturing continue to reduce hardware cost and complexity. This creates many opportunities and challenges for new profitable IoT services to be developed that were unimaginable just a few years ago.

IoT differs from traditional IT solutions in that the services typically include the deployment and management of large volumes of communicating devices. This presents many new challenges for business owners wishing to develop IoT services. There is a wealth of information available to support this development, but too often it focusses on the technology aspects and can offer confusing or conflicting messages. That, coupled with the fact that technology is changing so rapidly, means that what is written regarding IoT technology today may be obsolete tomorrow.

The focus on technology for IoT services means that the business aspects are often overlooked. Successful IoT services are built on a foundation of a clearly defined service offering complimented with operational and business models. There can be a tendency to treat each of these views in isolation, but successful IoT services develop these models in parallel.

PREFACE

According to Cisco CTO Kevin Bloch approximately 75% of all IoT projects fail due to lack of viable business experience. This book addresses that gap by offering the reader the possibility to understand a holistic view of IoT. It explains the business challenges and how they can be addressed, incorporating the technology and operational considerations. It is essential reading for business owners wishing to embark on their IoT journey.

Mattias Andersson (CEO MTek)

CHAPTER 1

Introduction

Internet of Things (IoT) technology is causing massive disruption across many industries with the pace of change accelerating daily. This presents major challenges for companies impacted by the IoT revolution, but with every challenge, there is an opportunity. Every company using the Internet will be impacted by the Internet of Things. Therefore, companies need to plan and manage their "IoT journey" to take maximum advantage of these new business opportunities. This book details the steps required for companies to successfully create, launch, and manage IoT services.

The genesis of this book can be traced back to 2017 when I was requested to host a series of IoT workshops in China involving several well-established IoT companies (and startups) with the aim to develop a strategy to rapidly scale their business. The challenge they faced was transforming their existing and new IoT services into a global, profitable, "as-a-service" business model. One of the companies already had more than one million devices connected but needed guidance to evolve its offering to enable global expansion and maintain a successful business plan. During these meetings, it was suggested I should document the concepts for other companies who were planning to launch or transform their existing IoT services to become more successful.

If you are impacted by IoT or about to embark on your IoT journey, this book will introduce the basic IoT concepts, the business implications, and how to solve the major challenges presented by the IoT revolution. While it does explain some technical aspects of IoT, it is not intended to be a technical book. This book will be useful to anyone about to embark

© Barry Haughian 2018
B. Haughian, *Design, Launch, and Scale IoT Services*,
https://doi.org/10.1007/978-1-4842-3712-0_1

on their IoT journey, including students studying IoT in university, IoT startups, and established IoT companies evolving their business.

The concepts presented in this book are based on actual business discussions with successful service owners, failed services, customers, collaborators, and competitors. Readers should apply the concepts to their industry sector and business scenarios, tailoring the recommendations to their specific IoT service needs.

I can't imagine anything less interesting than trying to read an IoT book cover to cover; therefore, this book has been written in a modular approach (akin to an IoT architecture). Each chapter can be read independently and could be considered for use as a module in an IoT training course, a topic for discussion in a workshop, or simply input for brainstorming exercises for companies working in IoT.

The Business of IoT

Many companies are embarking on their "IoT journey" because of business pressures to increase profits, corporate responsibility, social improvements, regulatory changes, or a combination of these. If we believe a small part of the hype around IoT, many will be impacted by IoT directly or indirectly. Therefore, a lot of current and future business leaders need to understand the business aspects of the disruption caused by IoT and how to take advantage of the opportunities presented.

A quick search on Amazon will confirm that most of the books on IoT are related to technology, and communication, with not enough focus on "the business of IoT." It is often seen as a technology revolution, but technology is only one of many tools to be employed by IoT businesses to achieve their targets. The most successful IoT companies are currently using, or will introduce, many of the tools presented in this book to create a successful, profitable, sustainable IoT business.

Two of the most important aspects I will discuss throughout the book are the necessity of creating ecosystems and delivering IoT in an as-a-service (AaS) business model. While these are not mandatory for success, they are useful tools that should be considered in all IoT business plans.

Ecosystems

Ecosystems will become the cornerstone for many IoT services to remain sustainable. I often describe this importance with the following sentence:

> *"For IoT to realize its full potential, it will require a series of ecosystems and currently non-cooperating industries to work together to maximize business."*

For example, there has been a significant evolution of energy services that now include smart meters using wireless telecoms communication. The question often posed is, "Are energy companies moving into the telecoms sector, or are telecoms moving into the energy sector?" I would suggest it's not important, but all companies should see this not as a threat to their industry but rather as an opportunity for new business and innovative revenue streams. This is an example of non-cooperating industries that can work closer together to increase their customer offerings. In other words, an ecosystem to create a more successful business.

The creation of an ecosystem for an IoT service should not be taken for granted. I was presented with a great opportunity for developing ideas to create IoT ecosystems by the master's program at the International Business School in Madrid. My team and I were given the opportunity to set a challenge for the students to solve concrete business issues facing IoT companies. The brief from the university outlined that the students came from a broad business background, some with a deep knowledge of IoT and others who didn't understand what the abbreviation meant. This was the challenge we presented:

"Develop an actionable plan for creating an IoT ecosystem."

I will present the results in Chapter 6, many of which can be used by IoT business managers to develop their own IoT ecosystem.

As a Service

It will be of no surprise to many working in IoT that another key message is that scaling correctly is fundamental to a successful IoT business. The business model best suited to IoT scaling is an "as-a-service" or "pay-as-you-grow" model. This means the price the customer pays is proportional to the usage of the service in terms of the number of devices or data throughput. Most successful IoT services will start small but will be designed in such a way that they can scale rapidly controlling costs and increasing margins as the business grows. In Chapter 9 we will look in detail at the management of the AaS business model and how it is perfectly suited to IoT services.

Before we start our IoT journey, let's take a brief look at how IoT has evolved and where we are today.

A Brief History of the Internet of Things

Defining the Internet of Things is not easy. There are as many definitions as there are "things." For some people, the "thing" is "everything." For others, it is "nothing." The answer is probably somewhere in between: it's "something." Kevin Ashton is generally credited with coining the phrase "the Internet of Things" to describe the network connecting objects in the physical world to the Internet.

The concept of a network of smart devices was discussed as early as 1982, with a modified Coke machine at Carnegie Mellon University becoming the first Internet-connected appliance. This Coke machine had the ability to report its inventory and whether newly loaded drinks were cold. The following encompasses most of the definitions:

> *"The Internet of Things is the network of physical devices embedded with software, sensors, actuators, and network connectivity that enables these objects to collect and exchange data."*

However, connecting devices to the Internet has been around for more than a quarter of a century, so why the hype now? One aspect is that we have seen major advances in technology.

- Hardware production has become more efficient in terms of capacity, price, and capability to produce the volumes required by IoT services.

- Connectivity capacity, cost, and quality of service have enabled more devices to be connected.

- Cloud platforms and IoT tools have become widely available, and usability has improved.

- Software production has been simplified with the introduction of tools allowing the rapid development of IoT applications.

Another major factor for the hype is that IoT is creating new business opportunities through innovation. The nature of many IoT services is that they are consumer-based, which is where a lot of the innovative services originate. The challenge to implement these services has decreased dramatically. In terms of cost, many of the most expensive technology components are widely available because of the growth of cloud services. This combined with the delivery model (usually an "as-a-service" model) enables many small companies to enter this space without requiring large investments.

Evolution M2M: IoT

For many, their IoT journey started with machine to machine (M2M) and evolved to IoT. M2M was on the hype curve five years ago, but did it realize its potential? The hype was certainly less than IoT, but it still fell short as many of the new business streams and use cases didn't materialize. One of the reasons for this is illustrated by a telecoms operator that created a new M2M department that built an M2M connectivity service. The delivery went very smoothly, and the product launched successfully; however, no one had posed the question, "How do we create a successful M2M business with new revenue streams from the service?" It was literally a case of, "We have a great service, but what do we do now?" The telecoms operator didn't know how to monetize on its M2M connectivity service and didn't understand how to attract enterprises to maximize the deployment. It was missing a business growth strategy and didn't understand how M2M devices and their associated data could be used to generate revenue. IoT has the potential to solve this via data reuse and the creation of ecosystems. I'll cover more of this in Chapter 6.

Data Reuse

Figure 1-1 illustrates one of the over-hyped aspects of IoT. M2M businesses are often based on siloes, and IoT will break down these barriers. The premise is that data will be reused, and it will become the key asset in the future. While this is true and is one of the keys for success in IoT, we need to cut through the hype and understand the real value of the data.

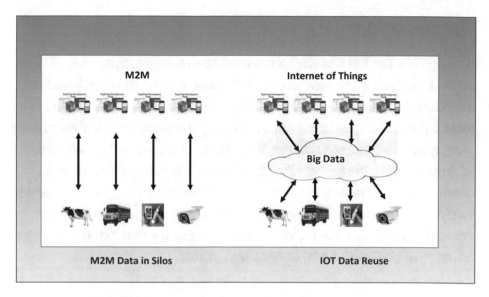

Figure 1-1. *M2M versus IoT*

I attended a meeting with an IoT partner who presented yet another "connected home" service in development. The presentation explained how their service enabled a fridge to communicate with an oven via a shared database. Almost everyone in the meeting nodded, agreeing this was very innovative and showed great potential. I decided not to point out that fridges have had communication capabilities available for more than a decade. Instead, I asked the questions, "Why do I want a fridge communicating with an oven? What value can I attach to a fridge communicating to an oven?" There was no answer forthcoming, as they hadn't developed a commercial business rationale for implementing this use case. My message here is that the hype needs to be controlled!

There will be new innovative ideas involving reuse of data, but they must facilitate the end goal. In other words, filling a gap in the market or solving an issue that creates new business and generates revenue.

7

The IoT Hype

IoT hype is great, but it won't last forever; therefore, we must take advantage of it in all presentations and discussions while it still benefits our business. It is an extremely useful tool for attracting customers and potential investors just by mentioning some of the astronomical numbers being quoted in numerous IoT articles. Figure 1-2 summarizes IoT device volume analyses. We can see the numbers vary significantly; therefore, careful analysis is required. See Ref. 1, "IoT Trend Watch 2017,"[1] for further reading. Part of this anomaly can be explained by considering how each report defines an IoT device. The numbers are so big that it doesn't matter for many of us if it will be 20 or 25 billion in 2020.

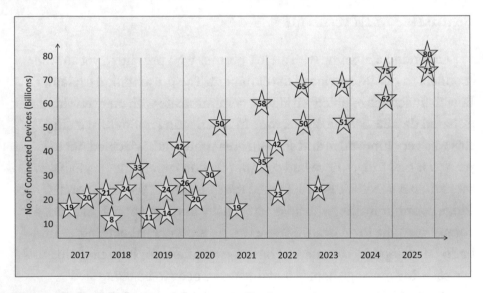

Figure 1-2. *IoT device volume predictions*

---

[1]IoT Trend Watch 2017. IHS Markit https://ihsmarkit.com/index.html.

We can see that we already have more devices connected than humans (see Ref. 2, "IoT Devices to Outnumber Humans in 2017"[2]), and we are likely to see an acceleration in device growth. Have we reached the peak of the IoT hype? It's highly unlikely; we are probably in a phase where many IoT service innovators and providers have their services well developed and now have the challenge of growing them into a profitable IoT business.

IoT is such an all-encompassing term that it can be more useful to understand the volumes within each industry vertical as each of these are evolving at different rates. In Chapter 8 we will look at this in more detail.

Conclusion

We will continue to see growth in the number of devices and the number of services. Many of the services will fail to become sustainable profitable businesses as they do not follow the fundamental principles outlined in this book. It's time to see that change; hopefully this book can contribute to the success of new businesses as they get started on their IoT journey.

---

[2]IoT Devices to Outnumber Humans in 2017 by Michael Alba www.engineering.com.

CHAPTER 2

Creating IoT Services

It may seem obvious, but the first question to be answered before creating an IoT service is, "What does an IoT service consist of?" In this chapter, we will follow the process of defining all aspects of an IoT service, as illustrated in Figure 2-1. For further information on the key documents mentioned in this chapter, please refer to the appendices.

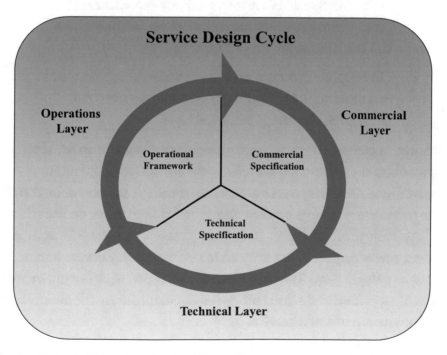

Figure 2-1. *IoT service design life cycle*

Many IoT service owners make the mistake of believing that the IoT service description and the technical components are sufficient for defining an IoT service. However, for a sustainable, profitable service, the commercial, operational, and technical layer specifications must be defined and recursively addressed as the business evolves.

The first step in creating an IoT service is to define an issue/challenge or business opportunity that can be solved by the service. The next step is to clearly specify the service so it can be understood internally by the service organization and externally by customers and collaborators.

- *Commercial*: Defines the service and specifies how it will be sold, detailing profits, forecasting volumes, and contractual terms and conditions (T&C)

- *Technical*: Specifies the technical implementation of each component and their interlocking interfaces with sufficient detail for life cycle management

- *Operational*: Specifies how the service will be operated and maintained according to the forecasts from the commercial layer and technical layer

Large organizations can turn the process of designing an IoT service into a document production exercise with too much being written, reviewed, and filed away never to be seen again. IoT services should start small (incubators in large organizations) and should never dedicate time and effort into producing non-critical documents. Figure 2-2 illustrates the documents required to specify an IoT service, many of which may consist of a single page. The key message here is that each document must be clearly specified and signed off by stakeholders during the design and implementation of a new service.

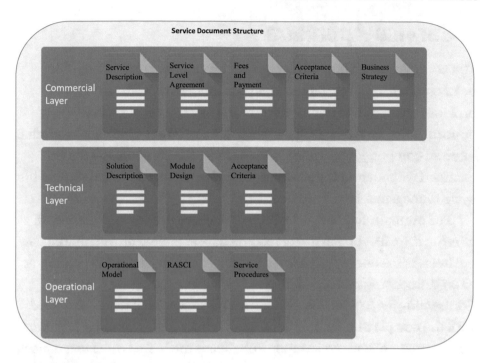

Service Document Structure

Figure 2-2. *IoT service specification*

As stated previously, the focus for the design of many IoT services is on technology, but this is incorrect. The first step is to define the service from a non-technical perspective. Customers may be experts in their industry vertical or come from a non-technical (IoT) background, so the service must be explained in their terms. The service description from the commercial layer should be a mandatory input for the technical layer as it describes the "what." The technical layer contains the solution documents describing "how" the service is implemented. When the technical description is available, the operational layer can be defined outlining the service delivery organization, with associated processes and tools required to operate the service. You cannot define how a service will be operated (operational layer) until you understand the components that should be operated (technical layer) and the budget available (commercial layer).

A Service Approach

The complexities of how the service is implemented should not be of concern to the customer. This puts more risk on the service provider compared to traditional product sales, but it also creates new opportunities. One advantage is that if the customers aren't aware of what internal components are used in the service, the components can be changed without requiring the customers' consent, and this simplifies life cycle management.

For example, IoT meter reading services are becoming widespread, offering the collection of meter reading data to energy providers. The core business of the energy provider is not meter reading data; it is producing energy. Receiving meter data is the issue they want to have solved. Contracting the IoT service means they no longer need to be concerned with the complexities of how data reaches their billing systems, just that it arrives on time. The service approach means the IoT provider can replace IT components, such as the databases, to reduce costs without consulting the energy company. Operation centers (that perform the daily activities required to maintain the service) can be consolidated or moved to lower-cost locations without impacting the service or consulting with the customer.

Commercial Layer: Service Definition

A commercial service is defined by the contractual documents signed between the service provider and the customer. In this section, I will outline the documents that are essential for a clear, contractually binding IoT service.

I will not discuss the sales material, which is part of the commercial layer, as this is service-specific. The majority of IoT services solve a problem that improves the top-line, reduces opex, or improves customer experience. These benefits must be explained clearly in the sales material. Often there can be a tendency to over-complicate the material, but my message is to keep it simple.

Service Description

The service description for IoT offerings is a contractual document that specifies service features, the boundaries of the service and how it is accessed. The service owner should approve the document and ensure it is maintained to reflect the introduction of new features and remains consistent for all customers. A careful balance must be drawn between making the service documents too detailed or too general without enough content. Too much content will increase the sales cycle, resulting in service owners getting bogged down with implementation details. Not enough will result in dissatisfied customers because of contractual misunderstandings.

IoT offers the possibility of collaboration between industries that would not normally interact. Therefore, it is critical that the service description is written using terminology associated with the industry vertical that will be understood by all stakeholders. Another frequent error is to write a service description as a feature description, but a true service model will make references to the delivery and operations of the service.

See Appendix A for an example of a service description; it should contain the sections shown in Table 2-1.

Table 2-1. *Description of Services*

Section	Description
Features	This section contains a high-level description of the features and functionality currently available. There can be a tendency to include technical implementation details in a service description, but this should be avoided. If necessary, the service components can be described in a generic fashion, but product names must be avoided. If the names of products that are used to implement the service features are included, it limits the flexibility of service providers to replace products during life cycle management. All attempts should be made to provide enough detail to instill the customer with confidence in the service while at the same time hiding the complexity. Note: If a product is well-respected in the industry (such as IBM Watson), it can be beneficial to state it is being used but do not include the name in contractual documents.
Initial Setup	This section contains the detailed steps required for the customer to get connected to the service for the first time. It can be as basic as registering a user, or more complex such as setting up a leased line for a secure VPN. The level of detail should provide no more than an outline of the activities required by all contributors. The customer must have a clear understanding of their activities and commit to executing these in an agreed timeline. Delays in execution of the initial setup can be critical as revenue is not generated until sign-off has been received from the customer.

(continued)

Table 2-1. (*continued*)

Section	Description
Service Access	This section contains a high-level description of how the service is accessed after the acceptance criteria has been met and the service goes live. It is important that this description has enough detail to enable new users to access the contracted features without requiring support. If the material does not have enough detail, it can result in operations being required to fill in the gaps and increases costs. For example, a clear specification of service reports and how they are accessed must be made available.
Service Boundaries	This section describes the service demarcation points. In other words, it specifies the technical limits of the key performance indicators (KPIs). For example, if the service is accessed over the Internet, the demarcation point could be defined as the router permitting access to service nodes. If there is an Internet failure but the router is active, it would be considered a failure outside the demarcation point of the service.
Service Security	This section describes the security measures implemented (without implementation details) providing a clear definition of responsibilities regarding security.
Optional Services	It is advisable to include a section offering add-on services and customizations. The implementation of these should be considered on a case-by-case basis and can become a useful additional revenue stream.

Service Level Agreement

The service performance is measured by the KPIs defined in the service level agreement (SLA). The key question for the service owner is, "What measurements will make the business successful?" Care needs to be taken that only KPIs that are important for the customer will be defined in the SLA. Other KPIs may be defined for internal use and never exposed externally. Where possible, the measurements and resulting KPIs should be collected and generated automatically. Manual generation can be costly and prone to error. These points are illustrated by the example of a meter reading service. Normally, KPIs are defined as how many readings (or percentage of readings) are available for processing at the end of each calendar month. If the SLA requires that 90 percent of readings be available the 1st of each month, the service provider should only report the performance at the end of each month. Measurements can be taken weekly to monitor progress and take corrective action (if the process is automated), but these are for internal use and not customer reporting. It may be interesting to measure daily performance to increase efficiency, but it should not be a KPI specified in the SLA. Other measurements such as how many readings are failing should be monitored, but again these are only for internal use. It is advisable to keep the KPIs defined in the SLA as high level and generic as possible. If they have a detailed specification, it can present additional challenges in terms of controlling how they are calculated to ensure compliance.

Another aspect to consider is to only define performance indicators that you can calculate, measure, and control. If the cellular network goes down, that will be outside the control of most IoT service providers. Therefore, you do not want performance measurements to reflect this.

Appendix B has an example SLA that can be used as a template.

Reporting Service Performance

Where possible, performance reporting should be available on a dashboard, and the production of the reports should be automated. If measurements and reporting cannot be automated, it can prove too expensive as the service scales in terms of resources and cost. A dashboard should be available to provide KPI measurements to reduce the quantity of reports and presentations toward the customer. As customers will always have access to the material, they can consolidate the reporting in the format they require and present it to their stakeholders. This is a method of pushing service operational activities towards the customer to reduce operational costs.

Customized reporting can be an important add-on service and is often given away for free. It is important that the service description has enough clarity to ensure the customer cannot request customized reporting free of charge. Sample reports with the reported KPIs should always be an appendix to the SLA.

Fees and Payment

One of the main advantages of the AaS model is that it provides a steady revenue stream rather than the peaks and troughs that can occur with product sales. This simplifies the financial control process that is linked to the sales forecasts.

The main issue new IoT services face is to ensure a constant positive cash flow. Therefore, the customer payment terms should be linked to the payment terms of externally contracted services. For example, if the IoT service uses a cloud infrastructure service where payment is expected within 90 days, then the customer contract should have a payment period of less than 90 days.

It is always best to incorporate an initial startup fee, but this should not be a one-off payment due when the acceptance criteria has been fulfilled.

It is better to define checkpoints that result in payments as the service installation progresses rather than waiting until final acceptance.

Another consideration for fees and payment terms is that IoT AaS business models imply a partnership with the customer. If the customer device volumes grow, their business is growing, and more revenue is being generated for the service provider. Therefore, the initial fees and payment terms should be agreed on with an approach to promoting growth, volume discounts, and so on. (See Chapter 4 for more information on commercial management.)

Acceptance Criteria

Often, acceptance criteria will be defined as a series of technical test cases that should be passed before the service goes live. For IoT services that are implementing an AaS model, this is not sufficient as the service provider takes full ownership of how the service is delivered and operated. Therefore, the service owner must take ownership of all aspects of the service, ensuring that the technical, operational, and business acceptance criteria are met. (Table 2-2 illustrates typical acceptance criteria.)

Table 2-2. *Acceptance Criteria*

Criteria	Description
Technical acceptance	A series of technical test cases to ensure all technical components are configured correctly.
Organization acceptance	A checklist to verify the service owner and customer operations understand how they should interact. It checks governance and working practices between the organizations are clearly defined and understood (may include training and certification).
Checklist	A final checklist to confirm all business, operational, technical, and training activities has been completed, with all service-relevant documentation released to the customer.

I was hosting a workshop with a multinational company in Germany, and they asked if they could review our acceptance criteria to check it met with their standards. They needed to ensure the service would be tested sufficiently before exposing it to their end customers. They were surprised to find the acceptance criteria included an audit and certification of their organization. They expected I would give access immediately as this was when we could start generating revenue. However, I explained an AaS business model has additional challenges. I wanted to ensure that they understood the service, how to get maximum benefit from it, and how to operate it successfully. Revenue is generated when the service goes live, but that is also when operational costs kick in. Customers who don't understand the service can cause additional tasks for operations because of an increase in the volume of questions, erroneous requests, or fault reporting due to misunderstandings. Each request results in an additional cost for operations and therefore will affect service profitability. Initially, this customer was quite taken aback by my approach, but it turned out to be a positive development as it increased their confidence in the service.

Business Strategy

The business strategy defines how to generate profits and is often the first point of failure for IoT services. Business strategies often include a market analysis, a marketing plan, a GTM strategy, deal types, and so on. This can be a never-ending library of analysis documents, most of which will add little value in making the business a success. Startups should keep their business strategy simple. Define the revenue streams and calculate the expected revenue by forecasting the growth plan. They should understand the cost drivers and forecast their evolution by maintaining (or increasing margins) as the service evolves. The service owner should review what is required for an effective business strategy and produce only what is necessary. As the service scales, the strategy will become more complex, but the fundamentals won't change.

All IoT business strategies should include a definition of the service revenue streams and the cost drivers, both of which are aligned with the sales forecast.

Service Revenue Streams

Revenue streams will be service-specific but should center on the core offering of the IoT service. What is solved by the IoT service? That is the principle revenue stream that is linked to the devices (or the data generated by the devices). This will be linked to the forecast and enables calculations to be made on the available income. It is input for other components in the business strategy that define how the service should grow in terms of features, devices, and customers. See Chapter 4 for further details on revenue streams.

Cost Drivers

There can be many cost drivers depending on the type service, but there are common trends in IoT services. The major costs are a service road map, operations, device manufacturing, service deployment, and cost of sales.

Figure 2-3 illustrates the major cost drivers that must be controlled during the evolution of a service.

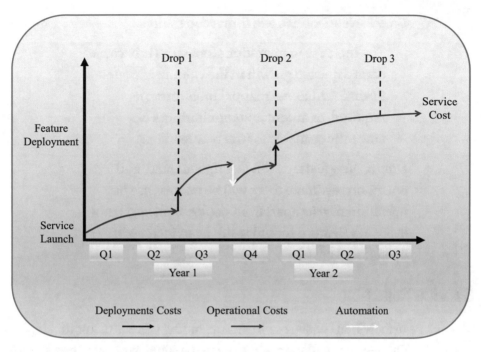

Figure 2-3. *Cost drivers: service evolution*

In this example:

- *Drop 1*: A new data center will be deployed because of new regulations or latency issues.

  This results in a major new cost because of a requirement to implement a new site. The cost driver is not only the expense of implementing a new site; it should include the recurring costs due to the operational support required, field services, and so on.

  There is an operational cost reduction between Drop 1 and Drop 2 because of automation.

- *Drop 2*: New features will impact operations.

  The increase in operational activities is because of an expected growth in the volume of trouble tickets. Additional manual monitoring is required, as automated monitoring is not currently available for the new features.

- *Drop 3*: New features will be implemented, and operations estimate there will be no increase in operational costs apart from deployment costs (not every new feature should result in an increase in operational costs).

Service Road Map

These are usually R&D costs, but in an AaS model it is a little more complex. The service road map will have two main drivers (customer requirements and the market conditions) resulting in feature proposals that require careful management. The evaluation process must be streamlined. It can be time-consuming in terms of costs and resources because of the analysis before acceptance/rejection (see Chapter 4 for more on requirements management).

A frequent error in estimating the cost of new features is to consider the implementation costs without considering the implications to operations. The cost of operating new features will be recurring and consequently can have a considerable impact on the business model. Another error in cost calculations is to omit the expected reuse of the features by multiple customers. Each new customer feature should become a central asset that can be resold to other customers. There may be no business case for developing a feature for one customer, but a forecast should be made of the expected reuse, and the development costs can be split across multiple customers.

Operations

The major transition many companies undergo while implementing IoT services is the deployment of an AaS business model. This requires that they transform an existing operations organization (or implement a new one), which can result in higher operational costs than those associated with a product/capex model.

The cost of operations will increase as the service grows, but it should never be a parallel growth. Figure 2-4 shows how the operations costs should remain relatively flat as the device volumes grow with the revenue. Operational efficiencies must be introduced through automation and consolidation, allowing the number of devices to increase while controlling costs.

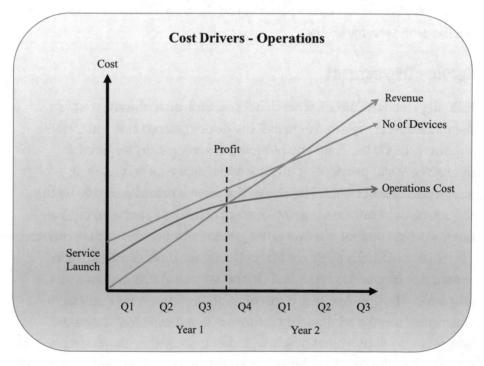

Figure 2-4. *Cost drivers—operations*

Operations is a major cost for IoT service models, but its calculation should not be related directly to the number of devices or even the number of customers. The operational cost will be related to the number of activities the operations team is required to perform because of internal requests, customer requests, support activities, internal maintenance, and so on.

Device Manufacturing

The majority of IoT service companies will have the production of devices outsourced, so this becomes a numbers game. As the volumes ordered increase, the manufacturer should reduce costs per unit, enabling an increase in margins. The value of the device increases with the value of the data; therefore, the business plan should show an increase in profits per device as the service scales.

Service Deployment

Industry trends for Internet services have evolved to the stage where the consumer is expected to install the device (sometimes with remote support). This is facilitated by reducing the complexity required for deployment and providing sufficient assistance via a service desk to offer support in case of issues. The aim of the service provider should be to reduce costs by outsourcing deployment activities to customers. The downside can be that revenue is not generated when devices are ordered or delivered. Usually payment is received when devices are active in the service central database, and (in this scenario) that depends on the customer. The upside is that it can often improve customer satisfaction. Customers feel the relationship is more of a partnership if they have control of the deployment process. Rather than feeling like a seller-vendor relationship, the customer becomes an active participant and contributor to the service.

Cost of Sales

Including cost of sales here may be a surprise to some readers. Many IoT startups will have a sales organization consisting of one person possibly performing multiple tasks. However, the planning of the sales budget should not consist solely of staff costs. There will be a travel budget, production of sales material, and most importantly service discounts. The service discounts are introduced by many IoT startup services to capture new customers and promote device growth. They can take the form of reducing revenue share percentages or the cost per device. It is usually more attractive in IoT AaS models as the revenue can be recovered over the full period of the contract. Commercial management should consider this in all calculations, balancing the short-term goals of increasing the customer base with the long-term goals of recurring revenue.

Technical Layer: Service Implementation

In this section, I will outline the technical documents required for IoT services. These documents should be mandatory, as they enable service life cycle management and differentiate a proof of concept (POC) from a commercial service. They must always reflect the current implementation and be of sufficient quality and detail for product managers, solution architects, and engineers to reference during the deployment and commercial life of the service for each customer.

Solution Description

The solution description is written by the solution architects (usually) from the research and development (R&D) and the DevOps organizations. It describes how the service functions are designed according to the specification in the service description. The solution description details the technical components, their interfaces, and a high-level

27

specification of their configuration. Normally, it will be reviewed by product management and the operations organization to agree on cost, implementation, and deployment methods. It will then be used by product management during the new requirements evaluation process and by operations during the implementation of new features and troubleshooting.

The document typically contains the following:

- Level 0, 1, and 2 architecture descriptions

- Physical architecture

- Functional components

- Interfaces and messaging flow diagrams

It can be shown to customers or partners but should be restricted to show only external interfaces and integration points.

Design Documents

The design of each IoT module may consist of high- and low-level design documents. High-level design documents can be omitted if there is sufficient detail in the solution description. High-level design documents will consist of interfaces and flow specifications, whereas the low-level design will consist of implementation details such as parameter settings, and so on. Operations will use low-level design documents to perform troubleshooting activities and check that parameters are set according to specification.

It should be noted that many functional components will be implemented across several modules. For example, there should be design documents for the security solution, which is implemented in all layers of the architecture and usually impacts all modules.

Operations Layer: Service Delivery and Operations

In the section I will describe the documents required to specify clearly the service delivery and operations organization including how it interacts with customers. For more details, see the IoT operational framework in Appendix C and the RASCI in Appendix D that can be used as templates for the documents described here.

Operational Model

The operational model described in this section gives an overview of how the stakeholders, organizations, and key players should interact by defining workflows and working practices. An AaS model is not a typical vendor/customer relationship, it requires that all stakeholders contribute to the success of the service by efficient cooperation. This implies that the operational model becomes more critical for the success of the business.

The operational model may not be necessary for startups but will become key for services as they scale in terms of customers and geographical location. The operational model used in many IoT services consists of a service management function and an operations function managing multiple customers following an ITIL/managed service model. The operations organization includes first-level and second-level support, as well as emergency management that follows strict guidelines and processes for managing operations. The purpose is to serve multiple customers using the same processes that become automated, creating an economy of scale.

The model outlines the expectations on each organization defining the interfaces with customers and collaborators. It should define the required formal agreements between organizations with an overview of the process flow. The following are the processes that should be documented:

- *Service management*: Governance on a management level including contract management, service scope management, and service performance reporting

- *Service assurance*: Defining how the organizations and processes are implemented to ensure the service is delivered according to the SLA

- *Demand management*: Detailing the operational flow for the organizations that implement internal or customer requests

To create maximum efficiency, the customer must understand the operational setup and the scope of the service. In a vendor-customer relationship, the customer will try to maximize service received from the vendor. However, an AaS model should be considered more like a partnership where a balance must be reached to provide a service where both parties maximize the benefit and the service provider is not punished by handling requests outside the scope of service.

Responsibility Matrix

If written well, the responsibility matrix can be a useful tool for service organizations, but too often that is not the case. It is a difficult balance to strike between making the RASCI too high level and too detailed. I advocate "less is more." It is best to have less detail and allocate high-level responsibilities than spend time discussing trivial minor activities. Too often one can encounter RASCI documents with hundreds of entries, and once approved, they are filed away never to be used again. The other extreme is equally bad: if the service organization is constantly referring to a RASCI document to understand roles and responsibilities, then it is quite likely that there are other organizational issues that need to be solved.

A good test for the quality of a RASCI is to review it several weeks apart. You might be surprised to find that your own interpretation of each entry in the first review is radically different from the second review. If that is the case, imagine how others will interpret it. You need a rethink!

Procedures Manual

The procedures manual is a structured template containing the practical details of how the customer and the service provider organizations will interact daily to facilitate smooth delivery of the service. During the customer initiation phase, this document will be completed to define the customer contact details. It will also detail the agreed governance procedures between the customer and service owner, including escalation procedures and reporting, and so on.

The process defining how the delivery organization will operate must remain consistent for each customer to facilitate scaling. However, the specific contact details of delivery managers, and so on, will vary from customer to customer.

CHAPTER 3

IoT Technology

In the previous chapter, we walked through the steps required to specify an IoT service. Now we will look at the technology options available to create IoT services. The most commonly deployed IoT architectures (the IoT stack) contain the elements in the reference architecture shown in Figure 3-1. The functionality is normally organized in a layered architecture with modules providing the specific capabilities in each layer. There has been an attempt to standardize IoT reference architectures by bodies such as ISO/IEC and ITU-T, but there is no clear winner yet. The options available can be divided into proprietary and open source platform providers. Examples of proprietary providers are AWS and Azure (focused on the full IoT stack) and others like ThingWorx (with more focus on application enablement). Examples of open source reference architectures are FI-Ware, OpenMTC, and so on. Complexities arise because each of the architectural options define their components (even devices, actuators, and sensors) in a slightly different manner. This creates challenges for IoT service owners to assess which are the best technology options for their specific service. The best advice is to keep it simple when deciding what is best for your service. Define the high-level requirements, specify clearly what functionality is required by each component in the architecture, check for compliance, and ensure it fits in with the business growth plan.

© Barry Haughian 2018
B. Haughian, *Design, Launch, and Scale IoT Services*,
https://doi.org/10.1007/978-1-4842-3712-0_3

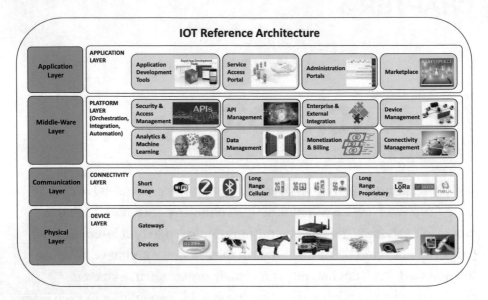

Figure 3-1. *IoT reference architecture*

The application layer provides access to the IoT services and interfaces with the middleware modules. The middleware modules implement the physical device/data modeling and much of the back-end data processing capabilities. The connectivity layer provides the communication capabilities between devices and/or gateways and the middleware layer's components. Each module in the architecture merits a book, but the focus of this chapter will be to provide a technical overview highlighting the business considerations of each layer and module.

Application Layer

The importance of the application layer can never be underestimated. It is fundamental to the success of IoT services as it defines how the customers access and view the service. An attractive, intuitive interface via an app or portal can be a useful marketing tool, increase customer satisfaction, and reduce operational expenses (opex). It is worth considering contracting design services for the graphical user interface (GUI) to avoid a common downfall for many IoT services, i.e., creating a GUI that looks like it was designed by an engineer and is neither intuitive nor attractive. See Ref. 3, "5 Keys to Designing Great UX for IoT Products."[1]

Figure 3-2 outlines the most common components of the application layer. Most IoT services will implement only some of these components.

- *App development tools*: IDEs, SDKs, and GUIs development software to shorten the lead time for creating the service interfaces

- *Service access app*: The end-user access point for the service; it usually consists of a service portal or an app

- *Administration portals*:

    Enterprise portal enabling customers to access the assets of the service, e.g. managing the sensors in an IoT-connected building

    Service provider portal to allow the owner of the service to add/delete customers, and so on

- *Marketplace*: An online store where the enterprises can manage, market, and sell services and assets

---

[1]5 Keys to Designing Great UX for IoT Products. IoT For All www.iotforall.com.

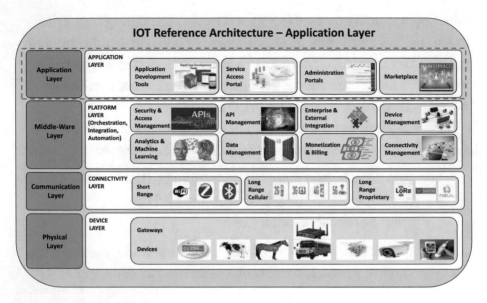

Figure 3-2. *Application layer*

The communication from the application layer is normally via APIs, using HTTP or Web sockets. The key message here is to clearly define the interfaces and ensure there is a clean separation between the application layer and other components in the service architecture. This is not specific to IoT; but a clean interface in a layered architecture becomes fundamental to control complexity as the services scales.

For a service to be sustainable, the service application layer should contain minimal middle layer logic such as analytics, billing, and so on. Adding logic to this layer results in increased cost and complexity for life cycle management. The modular approach allows for changes in the presentation layer (such as modifying graphics) without impacting other components further down the stack.

Application Development Tools

There are many application and developer portals with tools and services available on the market. They reduce the development time, complexity, and competence required for developing applications. The following are the key factors in deciding which tool is the most appropriate for application development.

Scalability

Do the application development tool costs increase as the service scales? Many of the licensed application development software tools require that the application is hosted on the server of the provider. This can prove to be an inexpensive option for proof of concepts (POCs) but may not be cost effective for a commercial service that expects to scale.

Functionality

Can the development tools support the road map, and will the costs remain within the boundaries of the business model? For example, many software development environments have optional tools that can increase costs significantly. If these are required for road map features, it can create unforeseen additional costs.

Prototyping

The main go-to market (GTM) model for most IoT services requires rapid POC availability. Customers will request POCs to be delivered within a short period of time to demonstrate the ability of the service provider to solve specific use cases. Therefore, the tools for the application layer must enable rapid application development and configuration for prototyping.

Sandbox

Can a sandbox (test environment) be easily implemented and maintained without incurring prohibitive costs? If frequent releases or upgrades of the service are planned, a testing environment will be fundamental. It will facilitate testing in a safe environment to reduce the risks of downtime and interruption to the live service.

Portability

Commercial application development tools often include features that introduce complexities when trying to port the applications. Portability must be considered as a road map feature if it is a requirement of the business strategy. Therefore, it will become a key requirement on the application layer software (other layers will also be impacted).

Integration

There should always be a clean interface between each module. If the interface consists of clearly defined APIs, this allows the IoT service to be cost effective for life cycle management. If considerable system integration (SI) work is required, it will prove too expensive to integrate and maintain.

This occurred during my investigation to migrate an Internet of Wine Service to an IoT platform. I discovered that the architecture and the implementation didn't match. It consisted of sensors reading soil and meteorological conditions that used Artificial Intelligence to advise on what chemicals should be sprayed and when to irrigate etc. After a brief analysis, I discovered that the application layer had been too tightly coupled to the platform layer. Therefore, integrating the application layer toward any IoT platform would have required considerable reprogramming and SI work. This was a case of bad design and would have resulted in considerable integration effort and cost that killed the business case for any migration of this service.

Service Access Portal

The access method for the service is likely to be a GUI via an App or Web page on a tablet, smartphone, or IoT device.

Before GUI design begins, there should be a business and technical analysis of which user interface (UI) framework to use, as it will impact development time and life cycle management. For example, if the programming language is Java, there are several options that can be considered such as Vaadin, Spring MVC, JSF, etc. There is a quite lot of analysis available on the Internet outlining the pros and cons, so a quick review should be relatively easy to do before software design begins. The correct choice can save considerably on development costs (see Ref. 4, "The Developer's Guide to IoT"[2]).

Common GUI

Implementing a common GUI for all customers is a key method to control costs and manage complexity during the life cycle management of IoT services. If the customer accesses the service via a web site, they will often request a portal with the look and feel of their company brand. Branding should be an option presented to the customer if it doesn't require a major effort. In Chapter 7, it is described as a professional service to be offered that can become a useful revenue stream. For example, as the service expands globally, there may be a need for multi-language app interfaces. Again, this is an additional service that should be charged for, as illustrated in Figure 3-3. The initial implementation cost for customized portals will not be the most critical factor to be considered. The ongoing maintenance is a recurring cost and can become significant for the period of the contract.

---

[2]The Developer's Guide to IoT. IoT Agenda https://internetofthingsagenda. techtarget.com.

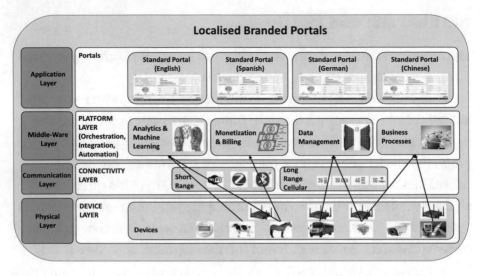

Figure 3-3. *Multiple-language portals*

Administration Portals

Typically, there can be two types of administration portals that are required for IoT services. The first enables the service providers to manage their customers, and the second allows the customer to manage their assets. These portals can be combined with different access rights and can deliver functionality as basic as a dashboard or as complex as advanced inventory management capabilities.

Service Owner Administration Portal

This is the access tool for the service delivery organization to manage the IoT service. The most basic administration portals, offer the ability to manage customer access rights, with more advanced versions offering access to billing, asset and workforce management functions. Requirements for this portal will come mostly from the service delivery and operations organization; therefore, it should not contain any customizations.

Its design is key for the service in terms of controlling opex, resource management, and complexity to facilitate the scalability of the service.

Customer Administration Portal

One of the major challenges for IoT is the management of large volumes of devices both by customer and by service providers. This customer administration portal enables each customer to manage their assets and access the service features. For example, if a meter reading service is being delivered to a water distribution company, they will need an efficient method to manage the devices and customers via their administration portal. The capabilities of the administration portal typically include service usage, asset configuration data, device status, and so on. The ease of use of this portal becomes key to the success of the IoT services. The ability to automatically generate this portal for new customers can be key for scaling.

Marketplace

The IoT marketplace is a digital distribution platform. It can serve as an app store for the enterprise's IoT applications, allowing customers to discover and buy supplementary IoT services and assets. Figure 3-4 illustrates an example of a marketplace that is often implemented for the service provider or the customer.

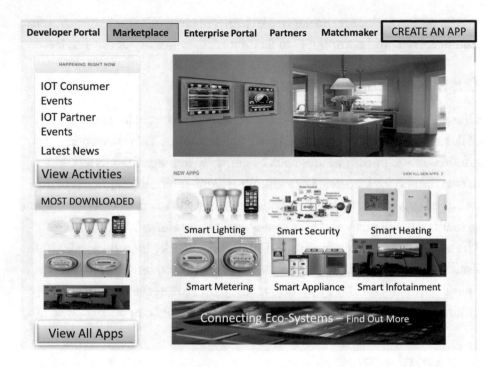

Figure 3-4. *IoT marketplace*

Service Provider Marketplace

Typically, as the service evolves, the provider will implement a marketplace to promote the service and sell new optional features. The most advanced marketplaces act as enablers for an ecosystem via the implementation of forums, blogs, and so on. A matchmaker feature can be a useful tool; it gives enterprise customers the opportunity to link up with other service providers and collaborators. It places the service provider at the center of an ecosystem and therefore central to the customer business.

The marketplace should be used as an environment to foster innovation, provide indirect support, give and receive feedback, and so on, supporting the evolution of the IoT service and its surrounding ecosystem.

Customer Marketplace

Customers' primary concern is that the IoT service addresses their use cases. However, the IoT service provider can add extra value to their customers by introducing new concepts such as an IoT service marketplace. If customers have additional services or assets that they wish to market, the service provider may be requested to implement and manage a customer marketplace. If this service is offered, it should be implemented in a manner to ensure it can be easily replicated and rebranded with the customer's logo and more. Otherwise, maintenance costs can become prohibitive.

Platform Layer

The service provider will require a middle layer or platform layer that provides the engine to power the IoT service. Typical requirement capabilities are data, device management, billing, analytics, business process management, and software development capabilities. There are many opinions regarding what platform capabilities are necessary for IoT services. In this chapter, I will use Figure 3-5 as a reference architecture to discuss the most common IoT platform capabilities.

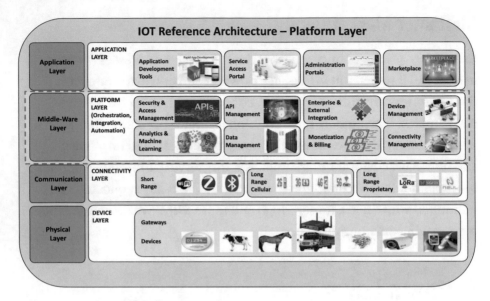

Figure 3-5. *IoT platform layer*

The service provider can choose to outsource the platform via platform-as-a-service (PaaS) providers, and there are many options available in the market (see the section "Outsourcing Layers and Components" for more information). It is impossible to generalize and rate one platform better than another as it depends on its suitability for each specific IoT service. The purpose of this chapter is to highlight the generic capabilities of each module and the associated business considerations.

First we need to consider that some generic topics that are relevant to any platform, irrespective of capabilities.

Public/Private Cloud

There is a never-ending debate over the pros and cons of public/private clouds, and a common misperception is that private clouds are more secure than the cheaper public cloud option. Unfortunately, it is impossible to generalize in this way, and the choice for each service must be analyzed on a case-by-case basis. The investment required for IoT providers to ensure their private clouds are sufficiently secure can be considerable. Public cloud providers have scale on their side and therefore have the resources to enable considerable investment in security. Private cloud providers are usually smaller with less expertise and resources to invest in security.

Often the solution will be to use a hybrid solution; in other words, the critical data is stored in a private cloud, and the non-critical data can be stored in the public cloud. This solution is often used when security requirements or regulations force the use of a private cloud.

Irrespective of the choice, it is important to manage customer perception of public and private clouds during the sales process and after the IoT service goes live. Most IoT services will include a shared environment, so it is important to ensure customer confidence that data security and integrity are maintained. Explaining the measures taken to protect customer data will be paramount for success (see the "Security" section for more detail). In the future, 5G will offer more possibilities for private networks via network slicing, and so on.

Finally, one should consider the costs as the service scales. Public clouds tend to start out as the cheap option but become less attractive as the volumes increase, whereas a private cloud requires more up-front investment, but the costs shouldn't increase significantly with scale.

Regulation

Government regulations may dictate the decision of a platform layer. In the second quarter of 2017, the Chinese government introduced a regulation prohibiting the storage of data outside China. This may not be a major issue if a public or hybrid cloud is used, as most cloud providers have data centers in China. In Europe, the mandatory GDPR regulations from May 2018 may have significant impacts on IoT services as they scale. The United States is also planning specific regulations related to IoT devices. Therefore, regulations must be considered in IoT growth plans, taking into account data sovereignty, and so on. Another factor is whether the service is planned to be sold to a public/government organization. The security regulations for these organizations can be more stringent, and this may have a major impact on cost.

A clear understanding of the regulations for the industry vertical can be critical for services. For example, IoT services such as Smart home or Smart metering that intend to launch in the European Union need to understand its specific laws regarding the data (which are constantly evolving). At first, it may be perceived that data cannot be exported outside country borders, but a deeper analysis may offer new options, allowing some of data to be exported with the provision that the data stays within the European Union and is anonymized. Anonymizing of data in this scenario means that the data cannot be linked to individual users (name, address, and so on), and it will be a prerequisite for many IoT services.

Quality of Service

Scaling globally can present challenges to ensure the quality of service (QoS) remains consistent for each deployment. This became the key issue for a service provider that had migrated devices from a data center in Malaysia to Europe as part of a consolidation process. The latency for signaling between Europe and Asia is considerable, and was noticed by the enterprise customer. However, a brief analysis confirmed it was not affecting the service delivered to the end customer. This is a clear case of where customer management comes into play. The enterprise perception was that migrated devices had a reduced QoS, but they were looking at internal performance indicators rather than the service provided to the end customer. On behalf of the service provider, we demonstrated that the end customer had an improved customer experience from the migrated devices. The latency did not affect the service negatively, and the focus from the enterprise should have been on the other issues affecting the service growth.

If there are issues with QoS, edge computing can be an option that should be considered, but this may increase cost and complexity considerably. We can expect edge computing to become more widespread as compute and storage costs decrease. It also emphasizes the need in many cases for considering a distributed design model. 5G promises a lot here, but in most cases if the distances are large, QoS will remain an issue.

Data Management Costs

Data storage and manipulation is key to the success of IoT services and is one of the major cost drivers. Contracting a platform layer with data management services is usually a cheap solution in the early stages of business development, but it can become expensive. Most platform providers charge according to the amount of data being processed. In other words, as device volumes increase, the data volumes and processing will grow in parallel. However, as the service portfolio evolves, the amount of storage and processing per device is likely to increase. A minimum target for the service provider should be to maintain margins per device as the data volumes grow. Many platform providers are offering cost models that decrease charges with data volumes in the service. For example, the first gigabyte processed will be more expensive than the tenth. Therefore, it should be possible for an increase in margins with volumes.

Another issue is the cost from platform providers for exporting data. Most offer data management coupled with additional platform services with the intention that all data processing is performed on their platform. They also increase costs for exporting data to external functions such as billing or analytics. Therefore, if there is an expectation that data processing may be required by external providers, the cost of exporting data needs to be in the business plan and road map.

During the service implementation phase for a transportation company, they explained a new requirement to stream and store video data for one year because of new regulations. They also wanted to offer the option that the data should be available for download on demand. This set the alarm bells ringing, as storing streamed data and offering it for export from a public cloud implied a significant cost increase. Therefore, the first calculation to be made was a cost analysis according to their service model, and it showed that a public cloud could not be considered as a long-term option.

Platform Layer Components

Now that we have reviewed some generic business issues, it is time to look at the platform layer components. A combination of these will be used to orchestrate most IoT services. It would be impossible to provide a complete "agreed" list of modules in a platform layer. Therefore, I will discuss the components that are the most critical or challenging for IoT service owners.

Security and Access Management

Security touches all layers of the IoT stack, but it is also a specific component within the platform layer. See Ref. 5, "IoT Security Foundation, Best Practice Guidelines."[3] The service provider is ultimately responsible for the security of all data received, stored, and exposed by the service. The service provider

---

[3]IoT Security Foundation, Best Practice Guidelines https://www.iotsecurityfoundation.org/best-practice-guidelines.

must implement secure access and identity management as part of their service or ensure it is provided by the platform provider. There are many security software providers available that cover all or several of the security requirements for most IoT services. Key considerations include logging users accessing data and monitoring of attempted breaches.

User Protection

The security level for users is one of the first considerations for service providers. The most basic security implementation involves providing a username and password to gain access to the service. More complex implementations are required when the personal details of users, including financial information, are stored. One of the more advanced techniques that is gaining popularity is a two-step approach that requires a user to enter a generated code sent to a phone or e-mail, but this may be overkill for many services.

API Protection

API security ties in with data protection. The information that is being passed via APIs needs to be verified and protected; therefore, authentication and encryption should be requirements on the platform service provider.

Device Protection

The platform layer needs to provide protection for the authentication of devices from illegal access. If the device is an actuator or smart device, illegal access could prove catastrophic. The platform provider should provide OAuth, OpenID Connect, or a similar authentication standard. Advanced device protection usually employs processes associating specific devices with users. One should also consider that each device in a service may require different security levels. For example, higher security levels will be required for medical devices than proximity sensors.

Data Protection

The minimum security requirement for data management in a platform is that it is stored encrypted. While this is fundamental for a platform provider and service owners, they should also consider packet data encryption during transmission. Implementing standards such as FIPS-197/AES to protect data while it is being transmitted is often overlooked, but these standards will become more widely used and relatively cheap to implement.

API Management

API management relates to the creation, analysis, usage, and their life cycle management of APIs. There are many products and services available for managing APIs, and these should be assessed in terms of flexibility, cost, and security. The minimum requirement for API management services is the ability to Create, Read, Update, Delete; however, there should be a consideration given to API mashups. Combining APIs to form new more complex ones can reduce messaging and processing power required to process the APIs. The key message here (that is too often neglected) is to define and manage an API strategy. APIs are assets, and therefore they should be planned and controlled regarding their exposure, their usage, and how they can be monetized. API management services should have the possibility to monitor API usage and capacity and facilitate monetization.

Enterprise Integration

The enterprise integration service can be classified as a professional service as it will involve a certain amount of SI. However, there are two key products that can be used in realizing the service.

- The Business to Business Gateway (B2B GW) provides the functionality to connect the service provider's software to external functions for the exchange of data. Usually, it implements standards such as XML or EDI that enable services to connect to multiple data sources. Almost all platforms provide this functionality, and they can be configured directly by the service provider. The minimum requirements should offer capacity management capabilities for sending/receiving external messaging and defining how data transactions are handled with the subsequent message flows.

- The Enterprise Service Bus (ESB) will be configured to communicate with other components in the architecture. The internal implementation of this should not be a concern for the service owner. They should provide the business flow with inputs/outputs, which will then be implemented in the ESB to automate the transactions between the components in the platform (see the example of the public train service in Chapter 7).

If an enterprise integration service is requested, the most important consideration is to ensure that the platform provider is actually providing the service. The receiver of the service should not have to allocate considerable resources, time, and effort understanding how the service is delivered via the SI activities. It should be delivered with minimum effort from the receiver and with most of the complexity hidden. There should be a clear definition of the inputs, as well as the interfaces, protocols, and activities required, before the service is contracted.

The activities and timeline requirements are critical for success in enterprise integration projects and should form part of the contract. The service receiver's first question should be, "How long will the integration take?"

Unfortunately, that can be impossible to answer. The integration activities from the service owner and the platform provider are interdependent. Therefore, the platform provider should define a critical path for deliverables in the integration plan and commit to their activities based on prerequisites.

Analytics and Machine Learning

The hype surrounding IoT is probably surpassed by the hype related to big data and analytics. For many, big data offers great business opportunities, but care needs to be taken as analytics can take on many forms and interpretations. It could be considered as basic as taking the average of two or more sensor readings. The other extreme could be a complex analysis of sensor readings using artificial intelligence techniques and historical data over the past ten years. The key message is that service providers should clearly define their analytics requirements before selecting the provider or platform module.

The most important aspects for analytics are the ease of use and visualization capabilities. Analytics is a function enabling business owners to extract information in a format that can be understood to facilitate business or operational decisions. Almost all the analytics providers claim to offer AI and machine learning without the customers understanding the benefit. The hype can be useful but if it's not needed, why use it? The most successful will be the services that provide an intelligent, intuitive interface that makes analytics easy.

During discussions with a customer, they requested if we could incorporate Watson into the service capabilities. My immediate response was, "Why is such a powerful tool required for basic analytics?" There are many analytics tools such as Watson with extremely powerful functionality, but it must be assessed if they are suitable for the service. If the current service or the road map requires the functionality provided by an analytics service, it can be a good match. Otherwise, it can be a case of using a sledgehammer to crack a nut. The cost of the analytics service must be analyzed within the service cost structure, ultimately ensuring it is generating revenue and profit either directly or indirectly.

During negotiations with an agricultural company regarding the implementation of their IoT solution, they requested that we implement their analytics functions in our platform. The company didn't understand that this was their key asset and should be protected. They had created an ecosystem of partners each providing components and data to create an agricultural service. What they didn't realize was that their competitive advantage and key asset was the analytical algorithms that could be used to improve productivity. Despite having a nondisclosure agreement (NDA), I advised that this should never be put in the public domain and should remain the key part of their solution that should be guarded carefully.

The real value from analytics is the knowledge the user can elicit to make decisions or take actions that add value to the business. The algorithms that create the analytical results are the assets that should be protected whether implemented locally or in a cloud system such as Watson or Power BI.

As mentioned, many analytics services are describing their service as including machine learning (or AI). While this might sound impressive, the reality is that complex AI is not needed and not provided in many cases. Ensure the service matches your requirements, and cut through the hype!

The more complex modules in the service architecture such as analytics and machine learning functions can be expensive to develop and maintain. It is usually not cost effective for a service to implement and manage this type of functionality for an individual IoT service. Therefore, they should be considered for outsourcing or implemented via partnerships. See Ref. 6, "Data Sharing, Advanced Analytics, and Success with IoT."[4]

---

[4]Data Sharing, Advanced Analytics, and Success with IoT. MIT Sloan Review https://sloanreview.mit.edu.

Device Management

Device management implies the modeling and control of devices that have been deployed in the IoT service. The implementation and requirements for device management will be device specific and depend on the business needs. Unfortunately, device management can be difficult to assess because of the many device types and inconsistent definitions. One should be careful not to assume functionality from the name; see the "Device Layer" section for further details on devices.

The key is to define the basic functionality for device management and elaborate on the specific service needs.

Typically, device management functionality includes the following:

- *Device control*: Configuration data for each device and how the devices are logically grouped

- *Device data*: Functions to support the management of payload data where it may be forwarded directly to other layers or modules

- *Data validation*: Basic functions to detect incorrect or missing values

- *Access control*: Management of access rights for devices to send/receive messages and store data

Provisioning

Most IoT services will have large volumes of devices; therefore, functionality to facilitate provisioning becomes key. Where possible, devices should be self-recognizing. In other words, they are automatically registered with the service when they are deployed. This implies a level of automation where the device will request a registration and authentication, and so on, when it is powered on. The ability to mass provision devices can reduce operational costs and complexity for service owners and customers.

A common requirement can be that devices are provisioned immediately after production to enable testing before commercial deployment. It can imply that features such as connectivity need to be activated. Therefore, a clear test strategy including prerequisites for device verification needs to be in place before deployment. It can prove to be an expensive exercise with customers in terms of finance and reputation if provisioned devices turn out to be faulty.

Remote Device Management

Remote device management can be critical if there is a wide geographical deployment of devices. Requirements may include remote capabilities for provisioning, software upgrades, and fault management. This will be useful for reducing operations costs as the device volumes grow. While it is not necessary to use one of the established protocols covered next, they can be efficient in terms of implementation and cost and are a useful choice to ensure future compatibility.

- TR-069 (Technical Report 069) is a technical specification that defines an application layer protocol for remote management of end-user devices. It was developed for automatic configuration and management of these devices by Auto Configuration Servers (ACS).

- OMA DM (Open Mobile Alliance Device Management) is a protocol designed for mobile devices. Security is via SSL and TLS cipher suites, but there is a lot of signaling for synchronization purposes. It is not suitable for large-scale operations with high-transaction rates.

- OMA Lightweight M2M is a protocol from the Open
  Mobile Alliance for M2M or IoT device management.
  A lightweight M2M enabler defines the application
  layer communication protocol between an LWM2M
  server and client in the device. It is suitable for
  low-cost, high-scale deployments with resource-
  constrained devices.

Data Management

Data management in IoT refers to the modeling of the data that the devices
receive or generate. Data management in an IoT platform is a middle-
layer module that receives, stores, and manipulates data. The data can
then be accessed on demand and presented via the application layer to
the customer (or other modules in the architecture). The modeling of the
data can be done directly by the customer via a data management tool in
the platform or data management offered as part of the service by the IoT
provider.

   One of the main considerations is to understand the regulations
regarding how data can be stored and managed and for what length of time
it must be stored. The data management function must comply with the
regulations at service launch and costs should not increase prohibitively as
new features are added.

Enterprise Tech cited a recent Gartner report that examined the
impact IoT will have on enterprise infrastructure. The report warned
that "due to a lack of information capabilities adapted for the IoT,
an estimated 25 percent of attempts to utilize IoT data will be
abandoned before deployment ever occurs."

Data management services should include as a minimum the following capabilities:

- Support data modeling to facilitate the aggregation, storage, retrieval, and presentation of data to modules in all layers

- Control integrity across distributed data repositories

- Control data security where it is exposed only to authorized components and users

These are generic requirements for data management and are meant to encompass an overall concept that the data should be organized well so that it can be easily stored, processed, and retrieved. The important aspect for the service provider is that the data can be retrieved and manipulated as the business requires. The processing of the data will be handled by other components in the platform layer that have been configured for the service. The service provider can assess the suitability of the data management functionality by judging the ease of use and flexibility of the data modeling.

Connectivity Management Services

IoT connectivity services normally refer to the communication management of the IoT devices as they send messages to other modules, layers, and devices in the service architecture. This offers the service provider the ability to have more control over their business by enabling the direct management of device communication (via portals and apps). The ability to receive the meta-data of the devices via connectivity management dashboards can be useful for business management and planning. For example, if a customer hasn't paid their bill or generated excessive data volumes, the enterprise could deactivate the device by limiting communication. The service often corresponds to the traditional M2M services offered, including connectivity management, billing, limited device management, and so on. Many connectivity management services offer sufficient capabilities to cover all the requirements for IoT services providing a cheaper option than implementing the full IoT stack.

Device connectivity is normally the responsibility of the customer/partner irrespective of the technology. IoT platforms should be connectivity agnostic and provide enough flexibility to manage connectivity and cover access types such as mobile, PLC, Wi-Fi, RF Mesh, fixed broadband, satellite, IP backbone, and so on.

Connectivity management includes the following:

- *Device access*: Users to have the ability to monitor device communication, e.g. the SIM card in a device or router.

- *Provisioning*: Users can order new SIM cards and activate/deactivate communication.

- *Billing*: Users can change billing profiles for devices or subscribers.

- *Segmentation*: Users can manage more than one type of connectivity.

- *Dashboards*: Users can track connectivity usage per device, geolocation, etc.

Monetization and Billing

The billing services offered by platform providers allow the service owner the ability to define how billing is performed toward customers, called *billing as a service*. The most basic billing model is to allow the service provider to charge per device, but more flexibility may be required as new chargeable features are added to the service. A frequent requirement is for automated billing to ensure operational costs don't increase as the device volumes grow.

If a service charges per device but some device types are using more resources than others, then more charging options will be required. Many service providers charge a fixed fee for all devices, but all devices may not be adding the same value to the service and not generating the same revenue. For example, if one device is streaming a lot of data and sending to a platform for storage but another device is generating 50 percent less data, should they be charged at the same rate?

The price per device in most cases will be dictated by the value to the customer (value-based pricing) and the cost for the service owner (cost-based pricing). Irrespective, the billing system must be flexible enough to handle these scenarios in an automated fashion. This may not seem important in the early deployment stages of a service, but the business model must be adhered to as the customer base grows with the possibility to implement individual charging plans for each customer.

Many customers may request reporting and billing is produced with a direct integration to their billing systems. This should be considered as a premium service and charged for in most cases.

One should also consider the effort required to produce customized billing or billing reports, as it is likely the requests for this add-on service will increase as the customer base grows. DevOps should analyze the impact to the service, keeping in mind that customizing introduces complexities for scaling and therefore needs to be handled separately from the central business model.

Communication Layer

The communication layer defines how the IoT devices will transmit the data between each other to be used by other components in the service. It is one of the lower layers in the IoT stack, and it presents most of the challenges to service owners in terms of complexity and business impact. For example, modifying an IoT service portal will be much easier than changing the connectivity solution for one million deployed devices. One of the first misperceptions to correct is to assume only one communication option should be deployed in the service. The service owner must perform a careful analysis of all options for the types of data that will be transmitted before selecting the most appropriate connectivity services.

In this section, I will discuss the suitability of the major connectivity options and their corresponding use cases, as outlined in Figure 3-6. Connectivity can be broken down into many categories. I will use short range, cellular, and LWPA. Each category has common characteristics that can make the choice between each relatively straightforward. However, the critical question to be answered is, "Which of the options within each category is best suited to the IoT service?"

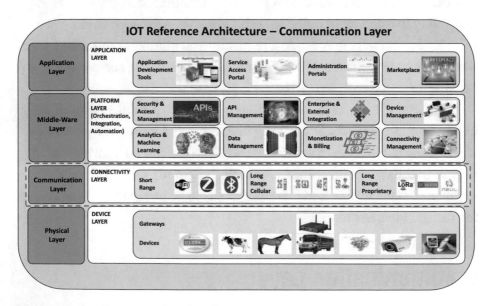

Figure 3-6. *Communication layer*

I will summarize the most common connectivity options available with their pros and cons, but I recommend further research before coming to a final decision on suitability for each service.

- *Short range*: As the name suggests, this is suitable for distances restricted to several hundred meters where access to the deployed device is not an issue. Many of the traditional M2M services use this option for short-range services. The main differentiator between short-range connectivity and cellular is the lack of guaranteed QoS. Many can testify from home use that Wi-Fi interference may occur by moving objects in front of the communicating devices. Short-range communication already has an extensive deployment in most homes or businesses and has a broad understanding in the market through Wi-Fi routers and Bluetooth-enabled devices. This may allow devices to be deployed into existing infrastructure, reducing cost and complexity.

- *Cellular*: For many IoT services that require longer-range communication, the preferred option is cellular. These are the traditional mobile phone connectivity services that can offer coverage in wide areas. Mobile phones and their networks were invented for speech, but they have evolved as networks for the devices. Data transfer is the most common use case for this technology offered by the traditional telecoms cellular operators. Many operators have been providing connectivity management services in the M2M space and now plan to move up the value chain and provide full IoT services. They are implementing their own IoT platforms or entering into partnerships with service providers that can complement their offering.

- The cost of cellular communication per device is the biggest obstacle in the IoT space, which is why telecoms providers are developing LPWA options. The operators are in a privileged position as they already have the networks in place, in other words, one piece of the IoT puzzle. Thus, the IoT revolution provides them with great challenges and new business opportunities.

- Although roaming costs are coming down, these can still be an issue for IoT service providers that are including cellular connectivity as part of their service. This is illustrated by my discussion with the representative of a very prominent connected car service. He explained that after the service had been launched in Europe, everything was fine until the summer months. The users started their vacations, and the cars started roaming all over Europe. This was a monumental error by the service provider, as they had to assume all the data costs resulting in a long hot summer of negative margins! Other factors that need to be taken into consideration for cellular connectivity are the taxes, data bundle packages, and increased costs for exceeding usage plans.

- *Low-power wide area*: This is the new player that maps well into the requirements for a lot of IoT services. As the name suggests, it provides low power across a wide area and thus facilitates the possibility for many industries to enter the IoT space without excessive investment. It can be split into the licensed and unlicensed spectrums, but I don't make that distinction. In many cases, it doesn't matter to the service provider. The key differentiators within this category will be made in terms of global reach, its scalability, and how the service provider expects the technology to match future requirements.

Figure 3-7 summarizes the connectivity options and their capabilities. These parameters are in constant change and vary depending on the environment where the service is deployed. For example, the communication range will be different for rural and urban locations. In many cases, it may be necessary to perform trials to understand the capabilities of the technology before mass deployment.

	Short Range				Celullar	LPWA		
	Bluetooth	ZigBee	Thread	Wi-Fi	2G, 3G, 4G, 5G	SigFox	NB-IOT	LoRa
Indoor Coverage	100m	300m	300m	1km	>10km	>5km	>15km	>1km
Outdoor Coverage	Low	Medium	Medium	High	High	<13km	<22km	<11km
Battery Life	1 year	1 year	1 year	1 year	1-2 Weeks	10-20 years	>10 years	10-20 years
Speed	1Mbps	250kbps	250kbps	1Mbps	up to 10Mbps	100kbps	20kbps	25kbps
Mobile Devices	Yes	Yes	Yes	Yes	Yes	Yes	Yes	Yes
Localisation	Very Low	Low	Low	Medium	Very High	High	High	Limited
Security	Very Low	Low	Low	Medium	Very High	High	High	Low
Future Proof	Yes	Yes	Yes	Yes	Yes	Very High	Very High	Very High
Deployment		High			Very High	Very High	Very High	Very High
Device Cost	Medium	Medium	Medium	Medium	Very high	Medium	Low	Low
Communication Cost	Low	Medium	Medium	Medium	Very High	Very low	Medium	Low
Scalability	Very Low	Low	Low	Low	High	Very High	Very High	Very High

Figure 3-7. *Connectivity table*

Short Range

Short range is typically used for services that require communication distances less than 300 meters using devices that communicate to gateways and hubs. In general, it is the easiest communication technology to deploy and manage, but quality issues can affect performance.

Bluetooth

This is one of the most popular short-range communication technologies because it is already available on many devices such mobile phones. There are several standards available: standard Bluetooth, Smart Bluetooth, and finally Bluetooth Low Energy. The latter is the most suited for IoT as it offers low-energy consumption and allows 127 devices to be connected, as opposed to 7 with standard Bluetooth communication. It is applicable for many IoT services via applications that want to connect to smartphones, smart locks, wearable devices, and so on. Version 4.2 via its Internet Protocol Support Profile will allow Bluetooth Smart sensors to access the Internet directly via 6LoWPAN connectivity. This IP connectivity will enable devices to connect with existing IP infrastructure to manage Bluetooth Smart edge devices.

ZigBee

ZigBee, like Bluetooth, has a large installed base because of its low power usage and low cost. It can be used to implement topologies such as star and mesh with a low transmission rate, and although it offers only short range, it can co-exist with Wi-Fi interference. It is best suited to IoT services that don't require large volumes and have infrequent transmission.

Thread

Many believed that Thread would become the successor to ZigBee as they use the same standard: IEEE 802.15.4. The main differentiator is that Thread has the capability of a mesh network. However, later versions of ZigBee have this capability without offering full IP compatibility. Thread is suitable for large volumes and infrequent transmission, but it is often seen as more complex to manage than ZigBee and currently doesn't have mass deployment.

Wi-Fi

Wi-Fi connectivity is often an obvious choice for many IoT services as it has a wide infrastructure because of it already having been deployed in many homes and businesses. In general, it is a well-understood technology and can be installed directly by IoT services' customers with minimal support. It is suitable for services that handle large volumes of data and require relatively high data transfer speeds. The downside is that it is power consuming and cannot be used in many IoT services where the devices are powered by battery.

Long-Range Cellular 2G, 3G, LTE (4G), 5G

Traditional cellular is suited to IoT services that require connectivity over large distances or geographical areas. It enables IoT services that consist of mobile devices to take advantage of the existing GSM/3G/4G (and in the future 5G) cellular communication networks.

Although cellular services can transmit large data volumes, reducing infrastructure needs, they are expensive and are not applicable for many low-cost IoT services. Another negative aspect is the power consumption required for transmitting over a cellular network. It puts requirements on the operations (field services) organization because of the need to ensure recharging and replacement of batteries occurs as required. Cellular technology is often deployed in data aggregators or gateways that receive information from sensors, as they can have a permanent power supply.

5G requires a special mention, as it is expected to be rolled out commercially before 2020 and should deliver a faster, more efficient network with lower energy consumption. It will offer many new features such as an increased ability to define private IoT networks (similar to private LTE). It will not be necessary for many IoT services, but with the quantity of devices and the volume of data being transmitted, it will become a useful enabler. Therefore, it should be considered for the IoT service road map to be implemented after the volumes have reached critical mass.

Cellular Features

It is important that the communication technology choice allows for maximum flexibility to match future business needs. New features available in the communication layer can be a differentiator, and cellular features are continuing to be developed, offering new opportunities for IoT services.

Cellular Portability

The importance of cellular portability features cannot be underestimated. Consider the scenario where a service has large volumes of SIM card devices deployed and needs to change operator because of an increase in tariffs. Cellular portability allows devices to change communication providers without swapping SIM cards or devices. Connectivity management providers are offering portability options to combat the cost of physically swapping the SIMs and the complexity of implementing features such as number portability.

SIM over-the-air (OTA) services allow information on the SIM card (including the IMSI number) to be changed remotely, enabling the possibility to change operator as the business dictates. Service owners should consider this a key requirement for the SIM card provider to ensure the SIM card type is compatible to implement SIM-OTA. There can be issues with the success rate of SIM-OTA deployment services. In other words, if a device is out of range, it cannot accept configuration changes. This can present challenges to the operations organization to verify if requested changes have been made. The inconsistent deployment of SIM OTA updates can impact the existing service, and this must be taken into consideration and mitigated against.

Virtual SIM is another technology provided by the operators that offers the ability to implement SIM technology without requiring a physical SIM card. The implications are considerable for global IoT services as it enables devices to be registered locally on the cellular networks where they are located. It reduces costs for devices that will be deployed globally and offers a global mobility without requiring roaming.

Another requirement the IoT service provider should consider for cellular connectivity is that the operator provides consecutive SIM numbers and ranges for the devices as this simplifies the management of large volumes of devices. For example, if a migration service is being implemented, it can be automated using scripts to work across IMSI ranges rather than individual IMSI numbers.

Connectivity Management

As described previously many traditional telecoms companies and operators offer connectivity management services based on M2M services via IoT portals. These services typically include device management, billing management, and subscription management, enabling enterprises to directly manage their assets and devices. These services can allow activation/deactivation of SIM cards, which is another way of implementing device management functionality. The services provided by many connectivity management providers may be sufficient for customers to manage their IoT offering and can provide a cost-effective solution where the full stack of IoT services is not required.

Other features that connectivity management providers offer are migration tools and services to remove the complexity of switching between cellular operators. These can also be used for generic database migration, increasing options for service owners with respect to life cycle management.

IoT/M2M Alliances

There have been several alliances formed over the last few years in the IoT/M2M space. These are currently quite loosely coupled but enable a global reach for many enterprises that previously was not possible. Their aim is to promote seamless international connectivity solutions for IoT and M2M services, most importantly providing unified business and operational processes through the alignment of their services.

GMA M2M and Bridge Alliance

Bridge Alliance is (currently) a mobile alliance of 35 operators (Deutsche Telekom, Orange, Telecom Italia, Telia Company, Softbank Mobile, Bell Mobility, Swisscom, and more) and thus provides a global footprint for services. It can offer seamless roaming that enables multicountry services. In early 2016, the GMA and the Bridge Alliance announced their cooperation to offer and deploy their advanced machine-to-machine multidomestic service across their combined footprint.

IoT World Alliance

The IoT World Alliance is (currently) a group of telecommunications providers (Telenor, Rogers, KPN, Telefonica, VimpleCom, Etislalat, Docomo, Singtel, and more) that can reduce the complexity of deploying M2M and IoT solutions. As the telecommunication providers evolve beyond pure connectivity, this alliance can offer global services with remote configuration and local connectivity using eSIMs (or virtual SIMs).

Low Power Wide Area

The technology choice for most IoT services will be LWPA, Its development is being driven by the requirements coming from IoT and it already has a global reach. The most common options are described below.

NB-IoT

The technology that most of the major cellular providers are opting for is NB-IoT as it has been designed to fulfill all of the expected requirements of IoT. It can be expected that it will be the choice for many IoT services as it provides good scalability, is low cost, and is reliable.

We can expect that due to its current hype/popularity, it can be considered as very future proof and should provide excellent global reach.

That is not to imply that it is the best choice for all IoT services. During a customer workshop, it became apparent the customer had considered only the NB-IoT technology for communication. If we considered this choice from a technology perspective, it was correct as it had sufficient radio range and communication costs were not excessive. However, the cost of producing the devices was too high. Therefore, I recommended that they investigate other communication options until the production price per device could be reduced to fit the business model. IoT device production costs will decrease as Industry 4.0 becomes a reality; therefore, we can expect NB-IoT devices will become more popular with low-cost services in the future.

Sigfox

This is a technology that was originally developed in France but is now being rolled out in major cities across Europe. It is a very power-efficient and scalable network, permitting communication with large volumes of battery-operated devices across areas of several square kilometers.

In terms of range, it comes between Wi-Fi and cellular and uses the ISM bands that are license-free. It offers bidirectional communication between devices transmitting data over a narrow spectrum. The premise behind Sigfox is that many M2M applications use devices that have small batteries requiring low levels of data transfer but can neither use Wi-Fi as the range is too short nor cellular as it is too expensive and consumes too much power. This option is useful for devices that are expected to be deployed for many years without requiring much intervention, typically ten or more. It is suitable for a wide range of IoT services that include smart meters, patient monitors, security devices, street lighting, and environmental sensors.

LoRa

LoRa targets wide-area network (WAN) applications. It is designed to provide low-power WANs with features specifically needed to support low-cost, mobile, secure bidirectional communication in IoT devices. As it is optimized for low-power consumption, the battery life is quite long, and it can support large networks with millions of devices, delivering with a low data rate. The cost per device should be cheaper than NB-IoT, but it does require gateways for communication, increasing capex and opex.

Neul

Similar in concept to Sigfox, this leverages very small slices of the TV white space spectrum to deliver high-scalability, high-coverage, low-power, and low-cost wireless networks. It uses wide-area wireless networking technology designed for the IoT that largely competes against existing GPRS, 3G, CDMA, and LTE WAN solutions. Data rates can be anything from a few bits per second and up and have a field life of up to 15 years.

Device Layer

This layer is the volumes part of IoT; Figure 3-8 illustrates some examples of what we can expect from the device layer. All the "things" in the IoT services will be devices with a wide range of capabilities. There are new forecasts on the volumes announced daily, and most of these will prove to be wildly inaccurate, but one thing is for sure, there will be a lot of devices!

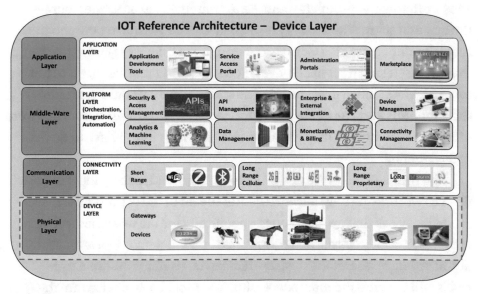

Figure 3-8. *Reference architecture: device layer*

The major challenges that IoT services must solve in dealing with such volumes will be the production, management, control, and communication of these devices.

I had an interesting discussion with Mattias Andersson, CEO of MTek, regarding how to handle the complexity and volumes of IoT devices. He presented an unexpected analogy between the Klondike and the IoT revolution. The Klondike is a gold mining area of Alaska that experienced a major gold rush in the early 1900s. Thousands flocked to the area and spent years working hard in their mines trying to strike it rich with gold, but only a few were successful. Some of the more astute businessmen had the idea of setting up commercial activities to support the mines. These involved services providing accommodation and restaurants with supply shops offering the products required for mining such as spades, lamps, timber, and so on. The analogy he explained can be drawn between the tools the miners used to extract gold and the IoT devices (and gateways) that are used to extract the data. The vendors and manufacturers of the tools (devices) had a guaranteed customer base; they could guarantee their margins and were able to introduce many add-on services. They were often the big winners, they had little risk, and they didn't have to do the heavy digging.

The message is that the design, manufacture, and management of the IoT devices will provide a significant revenue stream in the IoT business space!

IoT devices that are developed specifically for the use cases will be most successful in terms of performance and efficiency. However, it's about volumes; therefore, devices that can be used for multiple use cases will become the most successful. The most basic devices are the sensors that have capabilities to receive and distribute the data to other components in the IoT service. More advanced devices will also have bidirectional communication with the ability to execute actions based on the messages from other layers or modules in the IoT stack. For example, IoT agriculture services have sensors deployed that can send information related to soil humidity resulting in a sprinkler system being activated.

Devices

In this section I will discuss the key challenges and opportunities that service provider should consider in the device layer related to their design, manufacture and deployment.

Sensors

Sensors are the basic "things" that we are connecting in IoT services. They are the pieces of hardware doing the critical work collecting data. They are usually connected to each other via the Internet using a protocol such as MQTT or CoaP. They can be devices simply collecting data, actuators performing actions as directed by other components of the IoT stack, or smart sensors with some built-in intelligence. They are modeled in the orchestration layer by creating a representation that can send and receive the data from the physical device (or gateways). They are also the most repeatable object of the IoT business and therefore are fundamental for scaling.

The following are key considerations for the devices:

- Customizations should be kept to a minimum, and backward compatibility should always be maintained.

- Do sensors require data storage capabilities in case of communications issues?

- Are remote updates available to enable additional services to be deployed within the cost limitations of the business plan?

Gateways

Gateways are one of the consolidation points for devices because they allow legacy and new devices to connect to the IoT service. They may support one or several protocols and communication services to enable a common interface toward the rest of the IoT stack. Many have storage capabilities, implement edge computing, and facilitate the data flow securely between edge devices and the cloud.

There will be fewer gateways deployed than sensors; therefore, operation and maintenance of them is of less importance. However, there needs to be more consideration regarding their capability. The key criteria for considering the capability of gateways are the communication protocols, data storage ability, and edge computing to support current and road map services.

Communication Capabilities

Communication capabilities need to be understood and analysed during the design of IoT services as they can have a major impact on the business model. This became a critical discussion during a workshop on a connected bus solution. The customer explained a government requirement had been received that made it mandatory for streamed data to be stored securely for three years. The technical solution proposed that the gateways received streamed data directly from the bus via cellular communication for storage in a data center. The proposed solution resulted in substantial communication costs, killing the business case. We re-examined the requirements and proposed Wi-Fi communication; the bus could deliver the streamed data when it returns to the bus depot for free rather than implementing an expensive 3G solution to transmit data while it was being driven. Introducing a storage capability on the gateway allowed a new communication method to be used and reduced the overall cost of the service.

Capacity

Capacity and capability will depend on the use case and the growth plan of the service. The service should be defined independent of these technical requirements, but the capacity for managing the data flow and the number of sensors per gateway needs to be taken into consideration during solution design. For example, the deployment of a smart farming service with sensors would require several capacity calculations, such as the maximum number of sensors that can be connected to each gateway, the maximum number of sensors that can transmit simultaneously to each gateway, and the total capacity of data volumes.

The following are key criteria for selecting a gateway that ultimately impacts service cost:

- Number of sensors that can be deployed per gateway

- Data per message and the number of messages per second/minute/day/week

- Communication capabilities, what protocols it can handle

These are quite straightforward to calculate, but the analysis needs to be performed by senior engineers. Often, it may be considered a DevOps or engineering function as part of capacity management.

Storage Capabilities

Many services that plan to implement (near) edge computing will implement data storage capabilities in the device or gateway. If the gateway can consolidate data and intelligently send only required data to the central platform, it can reduce cost and complexity. In case of communication issues, it may be necessary for the gateways to store and retransmit data to ensure that service performance and reporting is not affected.

Single Processor Devices

A quick mention should be made of single-processor devices, with the most common being Raspberry Pi and Arduino. These are a cheap option for businesses that don't have the ability to design and produce their own devices. However, if the service is expected to scale significantly, this could become expensive. These devices consist of processors, RAM memory, Ethernet, or Wi-Fi for communication and a video controller. They are often used in universities for training students and provide most capabilities required for implementing POCs for IoT services.

Volumes

The cost of hardware and device production will continue to decrease dramatically, enabling new business opportunities in the IoT space. As the costs decrease, the volumes will increase, providing challenges to IoT services to produce and manage devices.

The Internet of Animals is an IoT service that "makes animals talk" via sensors connected to animals that can deliver the data on their health, eating habits, location and sleeping habits, and so on. This allows the owners to improve the animal welfare, increase productivity, and therefore increase their value. The challenge of how to scale the Internet of Animals was one of the first issues to tackle as the volumes projected were millions of animals, in other words, millions of devices. The production of these devices will require an innovative implementation of Industry 4.0 involving collaborative robotics, asset management, fault management, and operations management. It may come as a surprise to know that the designed solution requires one resource to produce one million devices per year.

Whether device production is handled internally or outsourced, the volumes dictate that production will require significant automation without much human interaction. If several machines are used in the device production flow, they will require the ability to speak to each other. This can be enabled via device and data management centrally controlling the flow of information. Automation should start when a new order is placed that automatically triggers a production process for new devices to be manufactured. This in turn triggers an automated business process that results in the delivery of the devices and invoicing. Automation should be considered for the full device production flow as well as individual processes.

Design

I was advising an agricultural company that wanted to implement an aggressive global expansion plan but didn't understand their key challenges to be solved. The first challenge we discovered related to their device production and inventory management. We noticed that each sensor had four screws and immediately suggested a device redesign. It sounds quite trivial, but when you scale this to millions of devices, it becomes an issue. The production, cost, logistics, and maintenance required to purchase and insert four screws in millions of devices is not trivial, but it wasn't considered by the service provider. They were quite bemused when the first redesign suggested wasn't for the circuit board or software, rather, a plastic casing. See Ref. 7, "Smart Cows and How Not to Design IoT Products to Fail."[5]

Device design is a skilled and complex activity that shouldn't be underestimated, but there are a few quick wins described here:

- Moving parts always will fail. If switches or buttons are present on the devices, there must be a forecast of a higher failure rate than devices with no moving parts. This is an important input to the operational and business plan.

---

[5]Smart Cows and How Not to Design IoT Products to Fail by Cheryl Ailuni. RFID Journal http://www.rfidjournal.com/internet-of-things.

- Device durability needs to be compatible with the environment. If there is excessive dust, heat, or humidity, this needs to be taken into consideration when designing the protection case for the sensor.

- The resistance to power surges, or electrical interference in the device operation, needs to be mitigated against if it is expected to be a problem.

Device Longevity

It is important to understand the lifetime requirements of the IoT device? If millions of devices are planned to be deployed, it is not feasible that they require a lot of servicing or replacing. They should have a long-life expectancy and a battery lifetime of ten or more years. Devices that are frequently transmitting data will have a short lifetime span. This implies that the amount of activity performed by the device must be optimized. If a device is deployed in a harsh environment, this will also impact the longevity.

Industry 4.0

The volumes of devices that are required for large-scale IoT services cannot be manufactured using traditional methods. Automation of device production will be fundamental to the success of IoT services. There needs to be optimization in processes to improve the production costs, simplified life cycle management, and a reduction on the reliance on human interaction (or as I describe it, interference).

Industry 4.0 is another revolution that is happening or about to happen in manufacturing. It combines the physical manufacturing with information technology to create what is often described as a smart factory. The manufacturing process becomes automated and intelligent. One of the more advanced examples of this is illustrated in Figure 3-9, providing a factory-in-a-box service delivered by an ecosystem of partners including MTEK, Nokia, and Fuji. It delivers prefabricated mobile smart connected device production factories that consist of the following:

- *3D printers*: Automated component production

- *Cyber collaborative robots*: Automated assembly

- *Artificial intelligence*: Optimizing the production process

- *Intelligent desk*: Interacting with robotics to assemble devices

Figure 3-9. *Industry 4.0*

The production process requires as inputs the device components, schematics, and robotic a program to assemble each device. The factory uses software to analyze the manufacturing process using AI techniques to optimize the device production. There must be minimal human interaction once production starts. Initially an operator is required for basic programming to assemble the first device and the design schematics for the components. This factory can be shipped in a container (and produce devices during transit) that has connectivity allowing remote control and monitoring. This enables the production of millions of devices with increased efficiency, increased quality, and immediate resolution of issues.

The aim is full automation of manufacturing processes. The deployment of the IoT service for a new customer should result in the automatic triggering of device manufacturing. The associated business processes such as logistics, track/trace, and distribution can be achieved with minimal overhead using these smart factories. All manufacturing should use this as a target to maximize production at minimal cost.

Implementing Industry 4.0 will increase capacity and reduce costs for device production; therefore, it should be incorporated in all device production IoT service road maps.

Life Cycle Management

IoT services with large volumes of devices or with a wide geographical distribution present considerable challenges for life cycle management. Software upgrades must be performed in an efficient manner and, if possible, completely automated. Take the example of how mobile phones upgrade firmware where the process usually requires a human to confirm the activity. Is this process suitable for large volumes of devices remotely connected with human interaction? Clearly, the answer is no. The devices must have the capability of being updated remotely without the need for human interference. That also implies a more rigorous testing process before upgrades are deployed and the possibility of remotely controlled rollbacks.

Automating the life cycle management of devices will reduce operation costs and increase performance, but it does come at a cost. Service providers should consider this during the design of the service and include automation activities in the road map.

We are very much a throwaway society, but a clear strategy is required to decide whether a device needs to be upgraded, repaired, or replaced. It's a business decision that will depend on many factors; the most important considerations are, how many devices are deployed? What is their geographical distribution? Can the activity be carried out by the customer, and what is the frequency required? Each of these factors needs to be considered during the design phase of the service with recommendations given to the operations team when the service is live.

Key Technology Business Decisions

The IoT service owner should have a broad understanding of the key technology challenges to be overcome during the design and life cycle management of the service. They will receive inputs from the business, technical, and operations teams before agreeing what, when, and how features should be implemented. This section will deal with the key technical challenges and their business implications for service owners.

Partnering Architecture Components

It can be a full-time job to analyze the possibilities of collaborations or partnerships with other IoT companies. In many cases I was surprised to find that offers came from current competitors who wanted to enhance their offering or increase their exposure and couldn't without some form of collaboration. This business scenario is not specific to IoT, but it is more prevalent because of the industry disruption caused by IoT and it requires the service provider to carefully evaluate partnerships. My recommendation is always to return to the fundamental question for the IoT business, "Will the collaboration help me connect more devices or improve margins?"

There are many reasons for entering into collaborations.

- A service provider may want to enter into a partnership by outsourcing layers or modules of their service if it proves more cost-effective. For example, if advanced billing capabilities are required, outsourcing can reduce complexity, reduce risk, and allow the service provider to concentrate on their core business.

- Collaborations will occur where there is a need for additional technical expertise, for example, if an IoT company has plans to expand to a new industry vertical. They may require industry-specific expertise that can be provided through a partnership deal without requiring recruitment or training that would impact cash flow.

- The global reach of a partner might be key. Many IoT platform providers have a great brand name and a global sales organization making them an ideal candidate for collaboration, especially with IoT startups.

- At service launch, capex is likely to be an issue. If the service owner does not have the capital to contract services such as PaaS, they can negotiate a revenue share model.

Negotiating with a potential partner who has an established service can put the service provider in a weaker bargaining position. This can result in one partner assuming too much risk, and the value of the partnership might outweigh the benefits. One method to mitigate against this is to share the risk in a revenue share model. The service owner gives a percentage of the revenue generated by each device to the partner. As the service grows, it can result in the service owner becoming very dependent on a partner, increasing business risk; therefore, it is advisable to have an exit strategy that is contractually binding. For example, if it is necessary to terminate a partnership, the service owner may need databases to be migrated. In this scenario, the service provider should have a contractually binding clause to require that databases are maintained and accessible to enable the migration after contract termination.

When a component from the IoT stack is purchased or outsourced, the IoT service provider loses control over the features from that module. They may have insufficient influence to request road map features critical for their business continuity. In general, a partnership should allow the service owner to have sufficient influence to ensure key features will be implemented as required. It is advisable to have contractually binding agreements for road map items offered by outsourced modules or layers before entering into partnerships.

Service of Services

It is not specific to IoT, but a good architecture allows for plug and play without a major impact to the overall service.

Figure 3-10 shows how a services could be constructed using only the modules that are required, enabling the service owners to manage costs and complexity by only paying for and using the necessary components.

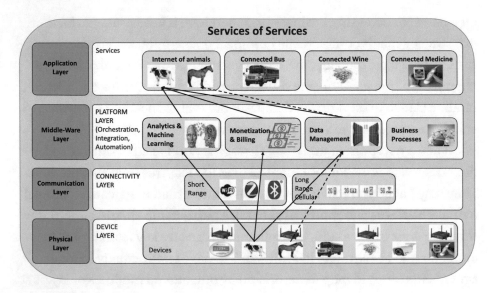

Figure 3-10. *Service of services*

As shown in Table 3-1, the Internet of Animals could provide two subservices, such as Connected Horse or Connected Cow services from an IoT platform.

Table 3-1. *Internet of Animals Example*

Animal	Service	Description
Connected Horse	Data management	Receiving animal health information
Connected Cow	Device management	Managing animal feed mechanisms
	Data management	Receiving animal health information
	Billing	Billing produced based on milk production

There are several factors to consider when planning to build a service from other services.

- *Components "as a service"*: Selecting subservices that are delivered AaS can simplify the delivery model and business management. If all components in the service can be contracted AaS, it facilitates cost management with respect to service growth. If some of the components must be bought as a product, you will likely pay for capacity that isn't required at service launch, and this can have implications on cash flow. Always negotiate payment terms for all products to match the business model.

- *Consistent SLA*: If each subservice has unique a SLA, this can present issues for operations. For example, if an external company is providing analytics services and their uptime service levels are different from a billing service, it will be important to plan for and manage this discrepancy. For example, if the Internet of Animals delivers a service level where the response is 24/7 for critical issues but the billing service provider only offers support during office hours, there may be a gap that needs to be bridged. It could be managed by contracting additional staff who are trained to manage billing trouble tickets, but a renegotiation to request 24/7 support is the best solution. Often it can be simply accepted as an additional business risk to be managed by operations.

Outsourcing Layers and Components

The strategy for outsourcing subservices or layers in IoT is crucial for success. The outsourcing options can be divided into the following:

- *Software as a service*: Providing access to software from a hosted environment

- *Platform as a service*: Providing access to middle-layer software components (See Chapter 7 IoT Enablers)

- *Infrastructure as a service*: Providing data-center access to host software

Outsourcing these components can remove a lot of the complexity. It can reduce implementation costs dramatically and critically reduce the time to launch. There are many options available, and they need to be given careful consideration as once selected, it may not be possible to change. There will be individual contracts with each provider, and there may be limited scope for negotiation as many of these services try to remain standard for all customers. The contract and payment terms should match as much as possible to the IoT service provider's commercial model, in other words, a pay-as-you-grow contract.

Software as a Service

Figure 3-11 illustrates SaaS providers in two categories, the industry verticals and the operational software, but they can exist for almost all components.

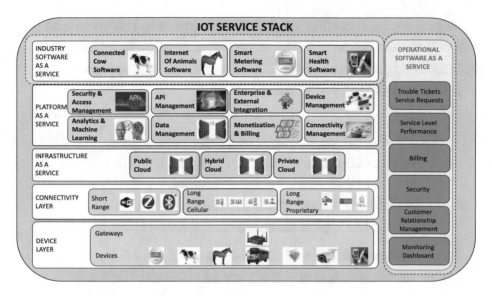

Figure 3-11. *SaaS stack*

Industry SaaS

In most cases the software from the application layer will be produced by the service owner as it is the layer that provides access to the features of the service. Where the industry-specific SaaS providers are contracted, it should be expected that they have a deep understanding of their vertical industry (and can demonstrate this). Apart from cost, the assessment should be based on ease of deployment, regulatory compliance, capacity, multi-tenancy, and road map features.

Operational SaaS

There exist Operational SaaS providers for every aspect of operational activities that one can imagine. The most common are project management, security, application monitoring, network monitoring, customer service and help desks. They offer SaaS solutions built specifically for every business function such as customer relationship management, business intelligence, and analytics etc. The options and associated costs can be quite daunting therefore very often the key is to only focus on the current service needs as there will always be options available to align with the service roadmap.

The following are the most beneficial categories for service owners:

- *Office suite software*: This is a suite of software that facilitates the execution of the daily activities of the service organization. The most common is Office 365 providing applications such as word processing, spreadsheets, presentation, e-mail, databases, and so on.

- *Service desk software*: This software facilitates the implementation of procedures for call centers or service desks. The service desk technicians assist customers who are having difficulty with the service. The software enables the users to register, filter, and track trouble tickets, directing issues to the appropriate support functions. The service desk engineers should have access to a service resolution database populated with a series of predefined steps to resolve recurring issues.

- *Reporting software*: This software enables the construction of dashboards to monitor service performance for customers and the service owner.

- *Security software*: "Security as a service" providers, such as McAfee, AVG, and Panda, offer a full range of security options, removing a lot of the complexity for service providers. The software can be installed locally but can be cloud based to support security monitoring for functions such as e-mail, encryption, and full E2E protection.

- *CRM software*: This software is used for customer relationship management and provides tools to facilitate the efficiency of the interaction between the service provider and the customer. It will often be used by all the functions of the service organization, storing contract details, sales information, and performance data. It may not be a cost-effective investment for startups but can be useful for IoT services that have scale.

Platform as a Service

Platform as a service (PaaS) is a cloud model that reduces the complexity in the design (and operations) of services by offering platform modules for use in the overall architecture. Reducing complexity increases speed to market and reduces development costs for services, making this an attractive option for many services.

Many of the IaaS providers have moved up the IoT stack to also provide PaaS services; therefore, if it is contracted, it usually includes IaaS. A key consideration in opting for a PaaS provider is that migration off the platform in the future may not be an option as it may not be cost effective. Therefore, choice of the PaaS provider becomes critical and must be considered during the initial the design of the solution. IoT services may be deployed on several platforms, but there needs to be a strong business case because managing a service deployed on more than one platform can significantly increase operational costs and complexity as the service scales. The business rationale is usually to attract new customers that already have software on a cloud platform, and it may prove beneficial provide access to a common database, and so on.

The following are the key factors in considering PaaS:

- Programming languages and SDK capabilities for software asset production (rapid application development)

- Sandbox features provided for new releases

- Administration of resources

- Pricing models for including the cost for exporting data

The choice between PaaS and IaaS providers can be illustrated by the following example. A company wants to develop a new connected cow service by developing an application and devices that could provide data to farmers to facilitate the management of the cows' feeding and drinking habits to maximize milk production. The service requires platform layer components that could provide advanced device, data modeling, billing services, and so on.

The options are as follows:

- Platform as a service enabling the components for device and data management to be configured and billing performed automatically from the platform. This allows the company to concentrate on the service implementation and not have to worry about the availability of these components or the infrastructure.

- Infrastructure as a service offering a data center with virtual machines to install 3PP software to be managed by the service delivery and operations organization. The advantage here is reduced reliance and collaboration on one provider for the platform layer components but increased complexity in managing the service components.

PaaS will be more expensive than IaaS, but it can prove to be the better option as it may permit a quicker service launch and require less technical competence from the service provider's organization.

Another common issue is when a service provider wants to export the data to enable complex analytics using its own (or the platforms) analytics software. The PaaS provider offering the most functionality may not be the best choice if the cost for exporting data is too high.

In both scenarios, the end customer who is availing of the connected cow service should not be aware of how the service has been implemented. The customer will be an expert in cows or milk production, not in IoT infrastructure and platforms.

On a final note, one should not underestimate the power of a brand name of a major platform provider as it can provide much needed credibility for startups. If a service is deployed using one of the major PaaS providers such Azure or AWS, it can be beneficial to highlight this in sales material using phrases such as "Powered by Azure."

Infrastructure as a Service

This service typically offers hardware services such as servers, storage, networking, and the floor space for the hardware. It is important that the level of service provided by the IaaS company covers the IoT service contract. For example, if the IoT service requires 24/7 guaranteed uptime, then the IaaS must comply with this. If the IaaS offers less uptime than the end customer IoT service, then the IoT service provider will be assuming the risk.

There are quite a few major players in this area such as AWS, Azure, Google, IBM, and HP all offering global deployment capabilities. It is difficult to differentiate on the service levels from each in terms of security, scalability, and so on, so often it comes down to cost. The calculations should be made for costs at service launch and the forecasted volumes. Infrastructure providers may be inexpensive in the short term but can become expensive as volumes increase.

If a smaller IaaS provider is used, security needs to be verified, and many of the following factors that are taken for granted with the larger providers need to be re-examined:

- Ease of use including monitoring and performance tools (for example, to manage capacity)

- Customer service (how the IaaS provider interacts with the service provider)

- Security monitoring tools and functions

- Is the IaaS provider compliant with the roadmap requirements?

If the infrastructure is not outsourced, there will be a need for an engineering function in the operations organization. This function requires a slightly different competence than the other layers of the IoT stack and therefore needs to be treated uniquely.

Distributed Design

One of the first considerations for the IoT services in terms of technical requirements is the possibility for a distributed deployment. This is necessary to overcome many of the issues related to quality of service, data regulation, and cost.

Often customers will have requirements for critical data to be held and processed locally in a private cloud. A distributed design allows for noncritical data remotely in public clouds to reduce cost and the critical data in a private cloud. For example, Figure 3-12 illustrates a service where billing and analytics data must be stored locally (due to regulations), but the service can be operated globally, and the data center location has no restrictions.

Distributed Data Centres

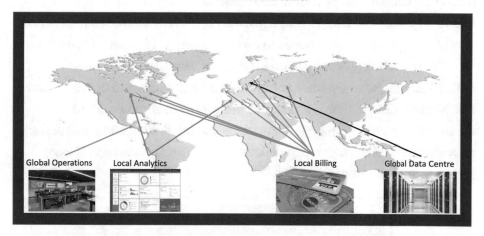

Figure 3-12. *Distributed data centers*

Distributed solutions present the following additional challenges that need to be planned for in terms of operational management and cost:

- *Communication*: Is there a QoS between the nodes that needs to be guaranteed?

- *Security*: What security is provided for each node and how is the communication between each secured?

- *Maintenance*: Life cycle management and fault handling complexity usually increases in distributed solutions.

The key message here is that all the data need not be treated equally, and this can help to overcome many customer requirements.

Multitenancy

It is essential to consider multitenancy options from the initial design of a service and its subsequent evolution. Often it is implemented by permitting multiple customers to use the same instance of the service, but it can come in many forms, and there are many solutions possible. It can be a high-cost driver and a primary requirement from customers; therefore, careful control needs to be exercised over its implementation.

Figure 3-13 shows several multitenant scenarios; irrespective of the solution, the customer should never be made aware of the implementation. This is not always possible, as they may want to understand how their data is secure in a shared environment, but service providers should always try to deliver toward the SLA and not discuss internal implementation details.

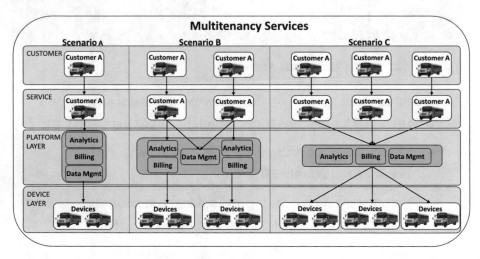

Figure 3-13. *Multitenancy*

- *Scenario A*: Each customer has their own instance of the service. In other words, there is a unique data center for each instance that has the software components uniquely deployed. This is not a true multitenant solution; there are benefits related to data security, and troubleshooting can prove easier than with a true multitenant service. In this scenario, the costs increase as operations are required to manage multiple instances, and there are no benefits derived from the reuse of infrastructure, hardware, and software.

- *Scenario B*: This scenario shows a reuse of infrastructure, but the analytics and billing components cannot be reused as they are not multitenant. The data management component of the service is multitenant, implying only one license is required for the software. Therefore, costs are reduced because of reuse, and there is improved scalability for this component. If there are clean interfaces between the modules and layers, this can be a good multitenancy option.

- *Scenario C*: This is fully multitenant where all components are shared by all customers. This provides most efficiency, but if there is an issue with one of the components, all customers may be impacted. Troubleshooting can be more complex, but that is offset by reduced complexity for operations. For example, if one instance is required for each component, then only one needs to be monitored.

Note that normally the number of trouble tickets influences the cost of operations; however, if the service is truly multitenant, one issue will normally impact all customers. Therefore, a trouble ticket may be received from each customer, but the issue needs to be fixed only once.

Scaling and Customizing in IoT

Scaling is the cornerstone for IoT services, and it needs to be planned by careful capacity management, maintaining a standard service, and managing costs. Business requirements often require IoT services to implement customizations. However, they should be kept to a minimum as the cost of producing and maintaining customized services negatively impacts scalability.

First, it is important to clarify what is meant by customization in an IoT layered modular service architecture. Unfortunately, I have never come across two service owners with the same definition. Often, it will defined as a deviation from the road map features that is not deployed to all customers. I will define a customization as "a unique software/hardware implementation or operational activity for a customer." It has no reuse value and won't become an asset to be sold for other customers. When a requirement is received from a customer, it should be assessed if there will be a possible resell/reuse in the future, this is a key input to decide whether or not it should be implemented.

Consider the scenario that a platform provider offers IoT billing services for new customers. The billing components will be configured according to the customer's charging requirements. That is a specific customer configuration of the standard product and therefore not a customization. The reason this is not a customization is that the assets are the billing modules, and their capabilities haven't changed; only the configuration has changed. If the software that provides the billing service is modified to fulfill the customer requirement, it should be considered a customization.

If a billing service produces a monthly report and there is a new request for it to be produced weekly, this may result in operations being required to manually compile the report. Therefore, this should be considered a customization. The assessment needs to consider whether it is likely that other customers will require this billing report with the same frequency. The short-term activities could be that operations need to implement the weekly production of the report. An automated long-term solution should be planned that may impact software to produce the report without any impact to operations. The deployment should be incorporated into the road map release plan, and the weekly report could be offered to other customers, attempting to standardize the customization.

In general, as you move down the IoT stack, the cost of customizations increases as does the impact to the business. If you customize devices or the platform services, it will prove too expensive to continue scaling. Typically, middle-layer components such as data management are likely to be used by all customers; therefore, any customizations to middle-layer software will impact operations and the business for all services. A customization to the application layer can be deployed independently of other customers, and therefore it is likely to have less impact on the business.

There will always be a continuous development of services and devices according to customer requirements. However, there must always be a business reason for every customization, and it should have minimal impact on the service road map. Therefore, it is necessary to consider the current and future expected impacts to the service. For example, if resources are allocated to managing customizations, can it impact the ability to operate and maintain future customers?

Security

Security is already one of the key issues facing services provided over the Internet. We all receive daily security alerts, and these will continue to grow in importance. Unfortunately, the Internet was not designed with security in mind! The first question for IoT service owners is, "What level of security is required for the IoT service?" This will have a significant impact on the investments required to protect the service and the measures required if/when breaches occur. See Ref. 8, "Keeping Cybersecurity Spending on Track as IoT Adoption Swells."[6]

---

[6]Keeping Cybersecurity Spending on Track as IoT Adoption Swells. Internet of Things Institute http://www.ioti.com (www.iotworldtoday.com).

Figure 3-14 illustrates one forecast for the growth of security for IoT services. The numbers illustrate that the growth in Internet security services will probably match the growth in IoT.

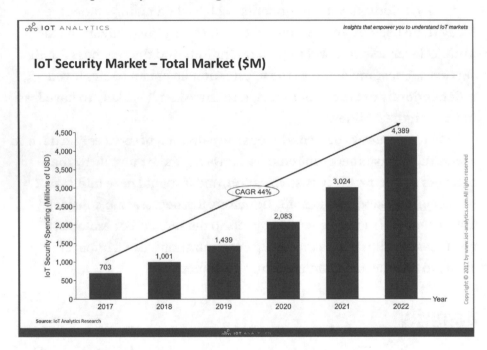

Figure 3-14. *IoT security business forecasts*

An IoT service that stores or processes customer personal information such as bank details will need a high level of security, whereas a sensor connected to a parking space can have a reduced level. It does not have to be expensive to implement basic security measures; however, it is important to define a security policy and include recovery actions in the event of security issues.

The main difference between traditional IT security and the IoT is the addition of device security; in other words, devices will access other devices without human intervention.

In general, the security policy needs to cover the domains illustrated Figure 3-15. If an IoT service has outsourced a layer or module, it must review the security policy and procedures by the provider to ensure they are compliant with the service requirements. For further reading, see Ref. 9, "Overcome IoT Security Challenges."[7]

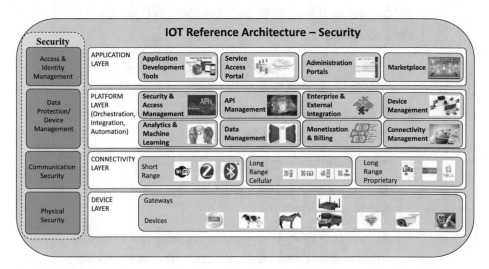

Figure 3-15. *IoT security architecture*

All these security controls form a unique combination of measures that protect the IoT service from the platform/device/sensor/gateway perspective. They cannot be treated independently, and one should keep in mind the chain of security measures implemented are only as strong as the weakest link.

---

[7]Overcome IoT Security Challenges. IoT Agenda https:// internetofthingsagenda.techtarget.com/.

Security Components

I will describe some of the key measures that will be implemented in each layer of the architecture, but an E2E approach must be adopted.

- Access and identity management covers all aspects of identity and access to IoT services including the following:

  - User access controls authorized users and levels of access to service components.

  - Login and password security measures should be implemented to restrict access.

  - 3PP session security measures for external IT systems accessing data or services should include monitoring.

  - Key and certificate management provides a means to implement and manage keys and certificates that are important security mechanisms.

  - Identity management and protection of stored data and while it is being transmitted is often overlooked and should be considered for all services.

- Middleware security

  - Data protection manages the security of the life cycle management of personal and secure data. It covers confidentiality, integrity, and availability of data at rest, in transfer, and used by the service.

  - Device management allows operations to detect and take actions regarding fraudulent/stolen devices or devices that are performing unapproved actions.

- API security is usually implemented via encryption and authentication, which will be fundamental for communication between all components. It is surprising how services do not have the most basic encryption even though it is cheap to implement and maintain. API communication control is usually provided by a layer 7 B2B gateway that provides full protection for XML and web service deployments against internal abuse and external attack.

- Physical security relates to the hardware, including infrastructure and devices.

  - Infrastructure protection covers the characteristics that are used to secure the platform both within the data center and at the data center itself. In general, data centers are ISO270001 compliant as a minimum, but there are other standards that may be considered, such as SSAE 16, SOC1, and SOC2.

  - Access to the infrastructure in the data center should be monitored and checked to ensure it is adequate, especially if it is a hosted environment with other companies.

  - Network protection looks at network-level isolation between different internal and external network segments. Server nodes and devices should be hardened to the comply with the service requirements.

- Virtualization security is required if software is implemented on a virtual machine in a cloud. It relates to hardening the virtualization platform and protecting the logical and virtual network structures by network level isolation.

- E2E security can be achieved by using generic bootstrap architecture (GBA). GBA aims at providing shared keying material between the service user and the device/sensor/gateway so that they can communicate securely.

Data Protection

It can be helpful to document a security policy as it will instill confidence with customers that security is taken seriously by the service provider. The data protection policies govern the management of the following security aspects:

- Data storage and transfer

- Disposal of media

- Privacy and stored data protection

The service provider is responsible for securing the integrity of all data attributes including the following:

- Analytics data

- Application-specific data stored or hosted on the platform

- Business process logic

- Charging and billing records including all billing metadata

- Customer relationship data

- Subscription data linked to the different users of the platform

- Transaction and payload data

CHAPTER 4

The Service Organization

The previous chapters outlined how the IoT service should be specified and many of the technology options that are available for its design. The next step is to define the organization required to deploy and operate a successful IoT service. In this chapter we will define the organisation and outline the key activities required to ensure the service remains successful as it scales. Figure 4-1 illustrates a reference service organization with the key roles required for an AaS business model. It is important to remember that IoT services should start small and grow fast. Therefore, the mapping of the reference organization for a specific IoT service can result in many of the roles I will describe consisting of one person covering several roles. The key for success is to define the critical activities and appoint an owner, in other words, someone who will be accountable for decision-making and managing the tasks required to achieve the business objectives.

© Barry Haughian 2018
B. Haughian, *Design, Launch, and Scale IoT Services*,
https://doi.org/10.1007/978-1-4842-3712-0_4

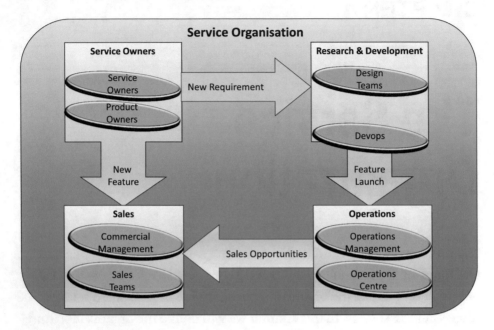

Figure 4-1. *Reference service organization*

The service organization consists of service and product owners who are responsible for the features and road map of the service. The R&D and DevOps organizations implement these features and hand them over to operations as they go live. Commercial management will decide on the pricing, and sales management will ultimately sell the service.

One of the keys for success is to ensure a clear governance between each of the service organizations. A frequent issue in scaled services is an unclear and complicated handover process for new feature releases that reduce delivery speed and increase conflicts between organizations. The service owner should specify the new features (including priorities) and manage the handover between R&D and operations. They should ensure the handover process is streamlined and involves only the sending and receiving organizations.

Service Business Owners

The business owner is responsible for the profit and loss (P&L) success of the service. They will analyze the inputs from all stakeholders and plan the business strategy, often balancing conflicting interests from internal organizations. Each organization will have their own set of performance targets that may negatively impact the performance of others but ultimately contribute to the overall success of the business. For example, a frequent request from the sales organization is for sales support from technical experts, but this can negatively impact operations or R&D deliveries.

Figure 4-2 shows a typical service organization, where the service is divided horizontally into technical layers and vertically into services. There should be roles defined that are responsible for the functionality provided by each horizontal layer (product manager) and another responsible for the vertical service (service manager). The product managers decide which products are to be used in each layer, and the service owners decide the functionality required for the end service. Note that Figure 4-2 is an example, and the structure will vary for each IoT service.

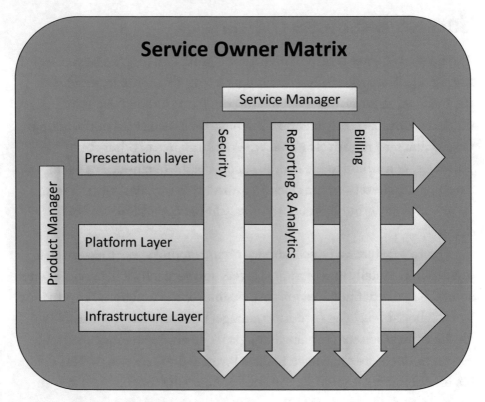

Figure 4-2. *Service owner matrix*

The business owner is accountable for decisions on new features and customer requests, but often they will delegate this responsibility to the service managers.

The service managers will define the requirements of the functionality delivered by the vertical service, and large organizations will often appoint several service managers. The product managers should have an overall technical understanding of the products under their responsibility (and their interfaces to other components). Again, large organizations may have several product managers appointed.

The product and service managers are key roles and must have a broad understanding of the service and the business requirements to be able to agree and define the road map that falls under their responsibility.

The example illustrated in Figure 4-3 defines how these roles should interact. In this example, the IoT service owner receives a request for a new feature that has just been launched by competitors, "Streamed data to be made available accessible from a dashboard." There is a further requirement that the data must be made available for downloading for six months and stored locally to comply with government regulations.

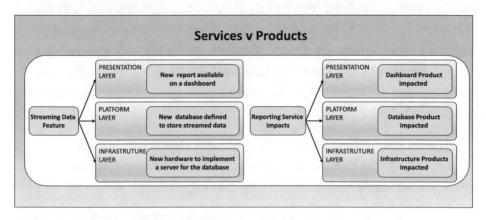

Figure 4-3. *Service versus products*

The reporting and analytics service owners discuss with the product (layer) owners to understand the cost and implications.

- *Presentation layer*: Impacted because of a new window being required in which to view the report

- *Platform layer*: Impacted because of the request to produce a report that contains a link to the streamed data

- *Infrastructure layer*: Impacted because of new storage capacity requirements

The service manager requests the product managers in each layer perform an analysis to understand cost and delivery options for the feature. The presentation and platform layers conclude it requires a six-week implementation plan that has no negative impact on current delivery. However, the infrastructure layer reports back a very high cost with an implementation project of 16 weeks and suggests an additional security analysis is required to verify security requirements are met for storing video data. These internal inputs along with the commercial aspects are considered by the service manager before recommending a go/no go to the business owner. The principal business inputs are the cost, the time, and the expected revenue, but others need to be considered, as described here:

- *Competitive landscape*: Are competitors providing the feature? Will it make the service less attractive if it is not available?

- *Operations*: What is the impact on operations in terms of cost? Do operations staff need to be trained?

- *Road map*: Will it have a negative (or positive) impact on the road map and current rollout of features?

These inputs should enable the business owner (or service manager) to make the correct decision regarding the implementation of the feature or for inclusion in the service roadmap.

The service roadmap should be available at the service launch as it provides customers with clarity to develop business plans and is a key input for forecasting service costs and organization dimensioning. If no road map is available, it can result in too many requests for new features that become very customer specific and make the service more complex to scale.

Sales

The sales organization consists of commercial management and the sales teams. These teams, with the support of the services organization (especially the service managers), will be required to produce a sales strategy accompanied with the sales and marketing material. This material is produced prior to service launch and should be lifecycle managed by the sales organization. Now we will delve into the specific duties of these organizations subsequent to service launch.

Commercial Management

The key task for commercial management is to price the service. They should start by calculating the cost of the service using several parameters, the most important being the cost of sales, deployment, operations, and development. They will price the service according to the forecasts, the current business landscape, and the required margins.

It is worth remembering IoT is a volumes game, and it cannot be successful unless the number of devices deployed in the service grows quickly. This can result in IoT service companies having very aggressive sales targets sometimes forecasting millions of devices. It implies large revenues and may place requirements for a large service organization to handle the expected volumes. If commercial management bases their calculations solely on the forecasts, they may decide initial deployments should be offered for free or with a negative margin to capture customers. However, if the forecasted volumes are not reached, there will be no possibility to recover the initial loss-making investment. In this scenario, it is important to renegotiate the service levels to reduce opex until the volumes reach the required levels.

Forecasts don't generate revenue! There should be a plan to scale the service organization, but it should be flexible enough to match the actual sales, not the forecast.

Service Deployment

The first decision that commercial management must make is what to charge (if anything) for the service deployment to a new customer. If commercial management insists on high margins for the initial service deployment, it can make the service unsellable. The other extreme is where the initial deployment is given away for free, negatively impacting cash flow. A common approach is to recover the cost of the deployment only; in other words, there is no margin. The revenue generated at service deployment is part of the business model, but it is not the end goal. The focus must be to get the customer using the service and growing it.

To mitigate against forecasts not being met, commercial management can employ several methods to recover the initial investment. A minimum recurring fee can be charged from when the service goes live, thus guaranteeing a minimum revenue and decreasing risk exposure. Another method frequently used is to charge with higher margins per device at service launch that decrease as the device volumes increase.

One of the professional services that enables a quick growth in volumes is migration of an existing customer base. However, analysis needs to be performed to ensure the migration can be performed in a cost-efficient manner. Customers may request migration be performed free of charge as the service owner can expect to recover the costs by the revenue generated from the migrated devices. The business calculations must ensure that the cost of migrating and the payback period fit into the business model.

Sales Teams

The most common issues I encounter with IoT sales teams is the change in culture required for an AaS model. It may not be politically correct to say, but it is often the case that the sales culture in a product sales business model does not suit an AaS model. Product sales are typically calculated

YOY with the bonuses being paid out according to the end-of-year figures. However, in an AaS model, the signing of a new customer may not generate revenue immediately or during the current reporting period. The AaS business model requires a long-term approach for the sales culture as illustrated in the example below.

Another issue to be solved for larger organizations is the scenario where a sales manager has a portfolio that contains products that are sold in AaS and capex models. The sales manager will be more likely to work to close the capex deals as their performance will be judged in current sales, not on the device growth that may happen in the future.

Consider the example in Figure 4-4 that shows an AaS sales growth starting with 100,000 devices per year and growing to 2 million in five years. A traditional sales bonus would be paid each year on the revenue generated by the current number of deployed devices, in other words, 100,000 for the first year. If the sales manager responsible for signing the initial contract moves to a different position after year 2, they will not be rewarded for the final size of the contract. Therefore, the reward structure for AaS sales cannot follow a traditional product sales model.

Sales Forecast Year 1-5

Year	One	Two	Three	Four	Five
No of Devices	100k	500k	1000k	1500k	2000k
Bonus	1k	5k	10k	15k	20k

New Sales Manager

Figure 4-4. *Sales forecast*

Several methods are available to create incentives for sales managers to adapt to an AaS culture. One solution commonly used is to continue rewarding the sales manager for the full period of the contract. Therefore, bonuses can be paid as the device volumes increase even if they have moved to a different position.

Sales vs. Delivery

Another major challenge not specific to IoT is the close cooperation of the sales and delivery organizations, but it does become more critical in an AaS business model. The contract signing in an AaS business model is the starting point for generating revenue, and the success of operations will directly impact the sales (device volumes) during the period of the contract. Therefore, the delivery and operations organizations must be fully aligned with the terms and conditions of the contract and be able to deliver the service as contracted. If the delivery and operations organizations are not delivering and operating the service as required, it will affect the device growth, in other words, the revenue. A good best practice is to give the organizations several common performance targets. This can help foster a better working relationship and ensure the ongoing development of common strategies.

Service Delivery and Operations

I define the delivery and operations organization as consisting of delivery management, an operations team, and DevOps. However, this is quite a simplified view and must be expanded upon for scaled IoT services. Many IoT services may consist of more organizations, but the minimum requirement should be that they include the fundamentals of the three organizations as described below.

Service Management

Service management is responsible for service delivery and operations; it can be divided into these two complementary roles:

- *Delivery manager*: A project-based role with the responsibility for all activities related to the deployment of new features, customers, and customizations. The delivery manager will hand over to the operations manager after customer acceptance has been completed and the service or feature is ready to go live. Project managers may report to the delivery manager who is fully accountable for the success of the integration and delivery projects.

- *Operations manager*: Responsible for ensuring that the targets defined in the service level agreements are adhered to. They typically handle the day-to-day operational performance issues and escalations to ensure ongoing customer satisfaction.

Services that have large deployments (in terms of customers or geographical location) might be required to further subdivide these roles into regional delivery and operations managers. For example, the world can be divided into three time zones of eight hours with a manager assigned for each region corresponding to their office hours, enabling 24/7 coverage.

As operations management must ensure the SLA is adhered to, they must be consulted on all new features. They should agree on a deployment strategy managing impacts to the service as the new features are deployed. In an AaS business model, the cost of the feature is calculated as the cost of feature development, deployment, and ongoing operational costs. Often operational costs can be overlooked, but the operations organization is almost always impacted by the introduction of a new feature or the implementation of a new customer. The product and sales managers must consult the operations manager to understand the operational impact, and the associated costs are controlled as the service evolves and deployment grows.

As service management will deal with the day-to-day delivery and operational issues interacting with stakeholders and customers, they should be the first escalation point for the local delivery organizations and customers. They can also act as a single point of contact (SPOC) to receive customer requirements and act as a filter before presenting them to the product or service managers.

Operations Center

The main function of the operations center is to monitor the service ensuring that it is performing according to the SLA and take corrective actions as required. The organization consists of engineers who provide monitoring and support services, offering a filtering and resolution function for service requests and trouble tickets. Normally it consists of first and second-level support and standardized deployment functions (see Appendix C). It is an organization that is built to handle scale; therefore, it is most effective when there is strict process control and standardized working practices. Many of the processes followed by this organization will be highly automated permitting increases in the device volumes without any major impact to the organisation.

Typically, the first deployment of new features requires the involvement of DevOps and R&D engineers to ensure success. However, there should be a plan to standardize the deployment activities, enabling future deployments to be carried out by the operations center when the process is sufficiently mature. Frequently, the operations center engineers can be promoted to DevOps engineers as they gain experience through on-the-job training working with customer issues.

Additional duties for the organization may include operational support functions such as change management, emergency management, and coordinating activities. The operations center normally interacts with customer care but may be requested to implement this function on behalf of the customer.

Development and Operations (DevOps)

DevOps is derived from "development and operations" and is one of the buzzwords for ICT companies. It is the amalgamation of software developers from R&D and senior engineers from operations into a new organization. It should never replace these organizations; it is complementary because it combines the best cultures from each to facilitate organization cooperation and to increase delivery speed and success.

DevOps is a key organization for IoT services as they require rapid release of new features, and many traditional R&D organizations cannot meet these requirements.

Implementing DevOps requires a culture change that needs to be understood by the development organization. R&D organisations normally apply rigorous development and testing procedures that may not necessarily lend themselves to short deployment lead times and frequent releases. The operations organization can be at the other end of the scale; customer and business needs often dictate their culture. It's a case of "just get it done" without sufficient diligence and testing.

A true DevOps approach includes development, operations, business owners, customers, partners, and so on. The collapsing of these organizations in a controlled manner will lead to great efficiencies in the management of the business and increase the chances of success.

The tasks of the DevOps organization should include the following:

- Development and release of features as mandated by R&D

- Technical support for requirements management

- Second- and third-level support for fault resolution

- Capacity management

- Security

A useful method for instilling the DevOps culture is to rotate engineers from R&D and operations in and out of the DevOps team. This develops a closer understanding between the DevOps engineers from a "slower" design background and the engineers from a "quicker" operations background. It can create conflicts, but if managed correctly, it enables DevOps to become an extremely powerful tool for success.

Research and Development

The research and development organization is the backbone of the service. It contains the experts who have the most knowledge of how the service is implemented. One of the most popular techniques used by the R&D organizations is Agile development using sprints. This technique aims to increase delivery speed (many would argue not necessarily the quality) and produces more effective results during the evolution of the service.

Why is this needed for IoT? The speed of change in technology is staggering. To quote Hans Vestberg, CEO of Verizon, "Change will never be as slow as it is today." The adaptability and speed required for implementing new service features will be a constant challenge for IoT service providers. Therefore, they must implement and adapt new techniques and evolve their organizations to meet this challenge.

Agile Development

Agile software development is usually defined as an adaptive, iterative, and incremental process to manage the development and implementation of new software features. Mature delivery organizations usually embrace this working practice very quickly, but it often requires a culture change as it promotes more autonomy and flexibility in delivery. The feature specifications are presented to the development teams, which are then divided into functional deliveries. The teams implement the functions, test, and verify with customers in an incremental process until full delivery has been achieved. As the customer is encouraged to provide regular feedback, it increases the possibility of success. However, it does require increased flexibility in the software development department to react quickly to customer feedback. The teams should be given the autonomy to adapt their development, testing, and delivery process as they are in the best position to understand how to increase efficiency.

Note that a common misperception is that the feedback comes from external customers, but a service manager should be able to give feedback on the functional deliveries as they ultimately must decide what is best for the business.

Scrums

Scrums are used in many Agile software development methodologies. They are most effective when used for software development of the application layer as it is most visible to the customer. Scrum teams usually consist of product (delivery) owners, scrum masters, and a (small) team of engineers. The scrum master works with the development team coaching and organizing the schedule and deliveries. The teams are self-organizing, managing the product feature backlog, delivery, and development processes working in sprints that should last no longer than a few weeks. The teams are cross-functional and must have the ability to define deliverables that achieve the overall delivery target. Scrums work best when the team is working closely and has the freedom and ability to adapt as the business requires. Quite often, it is suggested that the scrums deliver to the product owners, but the correct philosophy is that the team includes the product owners, and they together deliver to meet the business needs.

Requirements Management

Requirements (and road map) management is a process that brings the key players of the service organization together for decision-making and can be one of the most challenging processes to manage.

Figure 4-5 shows a typical requirements process. The entry and exit criteria for each phase should be defined with clearly stated expectations on each of the stakeholders.

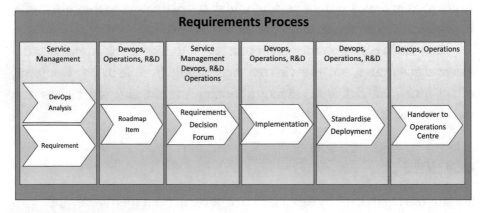

Figure 4-5. *Requirements handling*

The service management team should work with DevOps to structure requirements and assess the viability of each request. Subsequently, the requests get presented to the operations and R&D organizations for assessment. The decision forum is where the requirements from the customer representative (or business owners) are formally presented to the stakeholders to receive approval before being handed over to R&D (and DevOps) for development.

One of the common errors is that the teams and stakeholders do not allocate sufficient time to complete their activities in requirements management. Requirements management can be perceived as extra work outside their normal day-to-day activities, but if it is not managed correctly, it increases workload and frustration across the organization.

Business Support Tools

One of the main differences between operations for IoT and other ICT sectors is that they must plan for large device volumes. Therefore, the service organization will have more requirements on the business support tools to facilitate the management of these volumes, ensuring that operational costs and complexity are controlled.

The choice for operational tools should be based on ease of use, scalability, and automation possibilities. These tools will produce efficiencies that allow the operational costs to be kept at a minimum as the customer base and devices volumes grow.

Figure 4-6 outlines the categories of tools required by operations in a scaled service. In preparation for service launch, each service owner will have to analyze which of these tools are mandatory to manage the growth plan.

- Trouble tickets and service requests

- Monitoring layered architecture

- Billing and invoicing

- Service level performance

- Security

- CRM

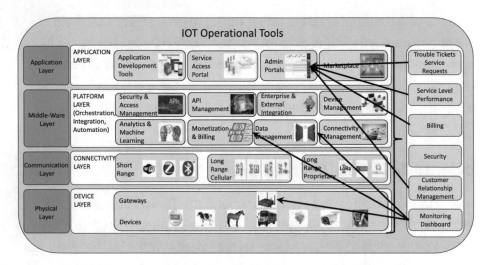

Figure 4-6. *Business support tools*

To maximize efficiency and reduce operational complexity, the DevOps engineers should create an operational tool architecture. It may prove too expensive to integrate all tools toward the modules in the service architecture. For example, the dashboard may only display information received from the billing and data management functions or, CRM management tools only need to interact with the service portals to facilitate optimized operations.

Trouble Tickets and Service Requests

Typically, customers will register tickets via an online tool as this is the cheapest method for handling support issues. The tool selected needs to be able to record, track, and report on the performance of registered issues.

The monitoring and performance of trouble ticketing is critical in IoT services as it can create significant overhead for the operations organization if it is not controlled. For example, if a customer has forecasted a quantity of devices being connected but this number has been exceeded, it may result in an excessive number of trouble tickets. While the increase in devices is positive, it can impact the performance of the support organization and negatively impact the perception of the service from the customers perspective. If device volumes and trouble tickets can be monitored easily, it can be useful in customer discussions regarding the SLA performance. Trouble ticketing tools can also be used to recommend improvements within the customer organization. For example, a customer may register what they believe is a fault, but the investigation concludes it is a misunderstanding of the service. Recording incidents such as these can result in recommendations for extra training for the customer staff to increase efficiency and understanding of the service.

If customers requests integration toward their ticketing system, it needs to be handled carefully. There should be no direct integration towards their system that involves a customization. The format for presenting/retrieving tickets should remain standard for all customers; otherwise, it will present too many challenges as the service scales.

Monitoring Services

The operations center will be required to manage the performance of the service by monitoring the individual service components, billing, analytics, and so on. The automated method is to have alarms generated by each component when there is an issue, for example, a server crashing that has been hosting analytics tools. New software or services usually don't implement automated monitoring functions in the early releases as they have other priorities. However, it should still be investigated what quick wins are available. Automated monitoring does not have to be expensive and can reduce operations overhead significantly. It can be as simple as a script pinging an IP address of a server to ensure it is accessible and flagging an alarm if there is no response.

Proactive monitoring will result in many issues being resolved without the need to inform customers but there needs to be a balance between the cost of monitoring the service and the benefits derived. It can create a positive perception with the customer if a fault that is impacting the service is reported before the customer is aware. However, if the fault reporting is automated (not filtered), it can result in faults being reported that may not be affecting service and therefore creating a negative perception with the customer.

Proactive fault reporting of the customer equipment can also be perceived as very positive. For example, if operations can detect and report that a customer server is not responding, this can lead to add-on sales and added value to the customer.

Billing Systems

Billing systems should be flexible enough to produce automated invoices and reports as required by the business. The adaptability of the system should allow several billing models that can be adapted for individual customers.

Service Level Performance

The automation of service level performance reporting may not be cost effective at the launch; however, it should be a road map item. As the service grows, there should be an automatic generation of the SLA performance for each customer as it will not be cost effective to produce manually.

It is often a surprise to many IoT service providers that I do not recommend it is available via a dashboard at service launch. It can result in many questions and escalations that should be handled in regular governance meetings. It is better that service performance is reported on a regular basis and discussed in a controlled format to maximize efficiency.

Security

Security measurement is a function that should be included in operations tools; it can be outsourced with many security products monitoring attempted security breaches and permit security issues to be handled internally before customers are impacted. However, it is unlikely there will be one security product that covers all layers, so once again, a balance needs to be struck between the cost of security with the risk to customers and the service.

Customer Relationship Management

There are several tools that provide different services within customer relationship management (CRM). CRM can be as simple as tracking phone calls or implementing an e-mail service, dashboards, project management tools, and so on. Many CRM providers show great cost reduction and benefits accrued by using their CRM products, but these are often only realized in mature services, so a cost-benefit analysis is needed. The tools provided by CRM suites often prove too expensive and difficult to create in-house; therefore, I usually recommend that they are a road map item to be outsourced as the business situation permits.

Key Operational Issues

Several times I have requested that IoT service management teams perform a risk analysis to understand what they believe to be the key issues that need to be addressed before a new service launch. The issue that is considered the biggest risk to the success of the business is operations. Further investigation usually shows that they don't have confidence that operational costs can remain relatively stable as the customer base and device volumes grow.

Operational cost drivers need to be understood and managed. Service owners should investigate the following activities that address the key operational issues (including costs) before service launch.

Customer Certification

Understanding the maturity level of the customer prior to contract signing is paramount to the success of an IoT service. If a customer doesn't fully understand the IoT service, they will not extract the maximum value from it, and customer satisfaction will be impacted.

Figure 4-7 illustrates a scenario too common in IoT services where customer 1 has an immature operations organization and is generating five times the ticket volumes of customer 2. They are only generating one-fifth of the revenue for the same service and are impacting the operational costs negatively. It is important to remember that each trouble ticket and request from the customer has a cost associated. Therefore, the service level agreement must include checks and balances for the service provider to address the volumes from customer 1. If their organization is not performing as expected, they should not negatively impact the costs for the service provider. A common approach is to introduce clauses that permit the service provider to reduce the response times if excessive requests are being received.

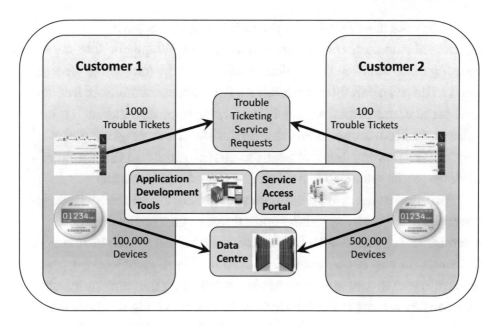

Figure 4-7. *Customer operations*

The best method to ensure that customers are competent to use an IoT service is to insist they pass a certification process. It can consist of training courses with tests to ensure the customer understands the operational flow and service features.

Even if customer certification is applied, the key is to ensure adherence to the service level agreement and control deviations. The operations manager has the responsibility to ensure customers are compliant and operational costs increase in line with the business model.

Training

Training material for IoT services is usually customer related explaining how to use the service via an App or GUI. However, as IoT services are built for scaling there should also training material developed for the customer and internal operations staff to ensure efficient ways of working are adhered to as the service scales.

If a service is well designed, the training and associated documentation costs can be kept to a minimum. Where possible, customer training material should be available online, but the format and structure need to be given careful consideration. For example, if there are frequent new service feature releases, it will impact the training material. It is an extra cost often not considered during the lifecycle management of a service. The training material needs to be structured and very modular so updates can be managed in a quick and cost-effective manner.

Technical training of operational staff can ensure efficient working practices and drastically reduce operational costs. The quicker the operations staff can identify how a customer request should be handled, the lower the cost to operations. For example, an efficient working practice is to train staff to investigate faults always following the same processes (e.g. the first activity is a database search) and allocating specific time slots for the investigation at each level before escalating an issue to the next level. See Appendix C for more information.

If the IoT service is being delivered (Business to Business) B2B, training can be a useful source of additional revenue. Providing training to customer staff is a high margin business; it can be sold to provide additional business or technical knowledge to customer staff, thus ensuring the customer understands how to create maximum value for their organization and customers.

Offshore Operations to Customer

Offshoring of operational activities to customers for IoT services can be a key tool to control costs. It may seem like a new concept, but it has been around for quite some time. Older generations of readers will remember queueing up at banks to perform transactions with bank tellers. Very basic activities such as checking your bank balance could be done only by tellers before ATMs and Internet banking were introduced. The introduction of ATMs and their evolution has enabled many banking services to be offshored to its customers. Now we perform most banking operations via the Internet or ATMs, and customer satisfaction has increased as we are no longer restricted to performing banking transactions during banking hours. Operations can be performed from anywhere, and we have more personal control over our finances. The bank has reduced the cost of operations and increased customer satisfaction.

IoT services should always have this in mind when planning the service road map. It is key to understand which operations activities can be performed by the customer via apps or web portals and which can be offshored without having a negative impact on customer satisfaction.

Offshore Deployment

Key to the success of IoT services is ease of use. If the deployment of devices is straightforward and can be performed by customers, it will be a key tool for controlling costs.

For example, if a customer orders a new batch of devices for a connected farm solution, it is better for the service provider if the customer can receive the devices by courier and they deploy to the animals with minimal remote support from operations. It is not cost effective for large scale services to have the deployment of new devices performed by operations staff.

Automation

This is often put at the back of the priority list for IoT service providers as it is often related to internal processes that do not necessarily affect customers. However, it is fundamental for reducing the cost of operations. There should be a budget set aside, and the level of automation should be one of the KPIs for the R&D and operations organizations.

For example, in a connected cow solution where each cow has a sensor, the central monitoring system can detect whether or not a sensor is reporting data. This can initiate an automated business process, where a new sensor is sent to the customer before they realise that one of their sensors isn't working. Operations costs for the connected cow solution will be minimized, and the customer will have the experience of a very efficient service.

CHAPTER 5

IoT Assets

In the overall IoT business model, great care should be taken to understand the value of the core assets, specifically, which assets can be exposed, shared, or sold and which should be protected. A clear strategy should be developed to maximize their value, and there needs to be a plan for generating additional revenue streams as the assets evolve and their usage grows. In this chapter, we will look at some of the key assets for IoT services.

Data

The Internet has given us incredible access to data that has now become an important asset previously not considered by many businesses. The search engines and social media groups have recognized this value and already monetize our personal data by storing search habits, location information, and so on. As there are already more IoT devices than people, the volumes of data will be incalculable and offer great opportunities for IoT services to monetize on the data being generated.

The value the device brings to the IoT business is one of the key factors in determining the success of the service. Its value to the business can be mapped to how the IoT service makes use of the data being transmitted to generate revenue. Innovation will be key to understand how to use the data and maximize its value to constantly create new use cases with their associated revenue streams.

© Barry Haughian 2018
B. Haughian, *Design, Launch, and Scale IoT Services*,
https://doi.org/10.1007/978-1-4842-3712-0_5

During meetings with a connected transport cloud service, we discussed a proposal to connect their gateways to an IoT platform for the collection of data from various traffic devices for traffic management systems. Their business proposal was that they would collect the data via their gateways and sensors, and it would be stored and managed in the platform layer. This data would then be exposed to the application layer as part of their service offering. Surprisingly, they suggested the platform owner could have free access to the data stored on their platform for other IoT services. They also permitted the platform owner to offer the data to other companies to develop new IoT services. The platform provider could also generate additional revenue streams if it didn't impact their core transport service. While this showed great initiative for creating a traffic management ecosystem, it also showed a complete lack of business knowledge of the asset they owned. The platform provider was hosting and manipulating the data, but they should not be allowed to reuse the data free of charge. It is key that the gateway owner should always have overall control of how the data could be exposed and used. For all IoT services, the owner of the data should always retain control to ensure they have the ability to develop new revenue streams.

For example, if a smart city service includes a connected traffic cloud that collects data from traffic lights, cars, parking spaces, and so on, this data becomes a key asset. The service owner can monetize on the data by implementing traffic congestion services. They may be successful offering this service, but have they maximized the value of their asset? No matter how innovative the service owner is, there can always be new ideas coming from many sources to create additional revenue streams. Offering the data for usage in an ecosystem (for a fee) could enable new ideas that the data owner may never have considered. In this scenario, the data owner needs to maximize the value of the asset by exposing the data and charging for its use.

A strategy for handling the data should be developed that includes a GTM model and a sales channel. I often recommend a marketplace because it fits into the concept of developing an ecosystem. As the data is already available, there is no extra cost except for capacity considerations; therefore, it is win-win for the company to expose and resell this asset.

The key question is how to value the data, and this will depend on the use case. Therefore, a revenue share model can be a good option. The service receiving access to the data pays a fee according to the usage and the revenue it is generating. See Ref. 10, "IoT: Harnessing Device Data."[1]

Data Reuse

Let's take the example of a utilities company that plans to roll out two million smart meters over a wide geographical area. For this example, we will estimate the cost of this activity at $20 million USD including the considerable cost of buying 200 trucks. Normally, a truck manufacturer will spend millions testing and analyzing the performance of their trucks, with data from brakes, steering, fuel consumption, and so on. If this data is made available to the truck manufacturer by the utilities company at a price, both companies can benefit. The business case for the utilities company changes as they are generating revenue from the data in the trucks; therefore, they can reduce costs for rollout of their smart meters. In this scenario, we have an energy provider selling data to a vehicle manufacturer, not something we would traditionally expect.

APIs

APIs (Application Programming Interface) are the most common method used for transmitting data and IoT service owners should develop an API strategy that is part of a service road map. It is essential both from the perspective of protecting a key asset and being able to monetize on it. The API specifications may be exposed publicly to help foster an ecosystem and demonstrate the capabilities of the service. However, it can be more

---

[1]IoT: Harnessing Device Data http://www.dzone.com.

beneficial to keep some APIs private if they implement knowledge or assets that are part of the IPR for the service. If the service provider plans to sell access to their API, they should select a value-based pricing model, in other words, calculating the value to the customer before setting a price as it will maximize revenue.

Algorithms

The intelligent logic contained in the service should always be protected as much as possible. This may consist of big data analysis, artificial intelligence, machine learning algorithms, or basic calculations that are perceived to be complex.

As mentioned earlier, an agricultural farm production service developed algorithms based on investigations into sourced historical data and the knowledge received from agricultural producers. The service owners believed their value to the market was the full agricultural service. However, they didn't understand the key asset was the algorithm. We were able to demonstrate that the other components of the service were easily reproducible, in other words, the application, devices, and platform layer components. The algorithms and resulting actions taken according the historical, meteorological, and chemical conditions were the key differentiators for the service. The service owner was advised to take steps to protect the algorithms before service launch, and access to them was provided under strict legal conditions.

Patents

The application layer should be implemented as a presentation layer, but that shouldn't imply that it is not an important asset. The application layer defines how the service is accessed. It is the showcase for the service and may contain features that are possible to patent. I was pleasantly surprised to find that many IoT services are patented. They may consist of components drawn from partners and suppliers that are packaged into an IoT service, but can still become patented. Many larger IT companies have departments dedicated solely to patenting, but this will not be possible for small IoT service companies. One option is to contract external specialist patenting companies to provide the required expertise. I discussed IoT patenting with a patenting consultant, and they suggested it will not be suitable for many IoT services because of the effort required to define the patent and the associated cost to protect it. The challenge with patenting is that it can be expensive to contract specialists to define and defend the patents in case of a suspected breach.

Devices

The physical layer of the IoT stack contains the devices and communication gateways illustrated in Figure 5-1, and the capability of these devices can become an asset to be resold. The device enables the mechanism for sending/receiving and possibly storing the data. Often, the value of the device is related to the data it delivers, so it should be considered as an asset that may generate additional revenue streams.

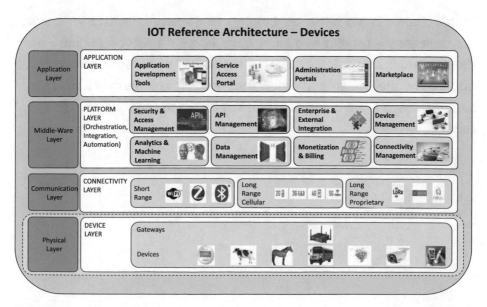

Figure 5-1. *Device assets*

Many consider the hardware contained in the device to be a key asset, but that will not be the case for many IoT services. The hardware is just a tool to communicate data and actions. While hardware capacity has been increasing at an accelerated rate for many decades, costs have gone in the other direction. In most cases, hardware loses its value quickly, so its real value to the business is via the data it is delivering.

I was meeting a device production company in China and was surprised that they were openly displaying and explaining the internal design of their devices. When I questioned this approach, they explained that it is not difficult to copy device design; therefore, they did not consider it an asset. What they did consider as their key asset was creating an open environment to discuss device design as they attempted to attract new customers. They planned to create an open ecosystem environment around the company, and the devices were part of that plan.

Manage IoT Assets

In this chapter I have introduced many of the assets defined in IoT services, but each service is unique and may have different assets other than those mentioned previously. The key message is that IoT services must understand their assets and expect their value to change over time. The careful management of assets will be key for the longevity of each IoT service.

CHAPTER 6

IoT Ecosystems

What is an IoT ecosystem? It may surprise you to know there are as many definitions as there are ecosystems. An IoT ecosystem is often defined as the collaborators involved in the development and evolution of IoT services. What is usually missing from this definition are the users of the service who are fundamental for its evolution and its surrounding ecosystem.

Ecosystems are fundamental for the success in the IoT because of the diversity of technologies and industries involved in creating services, as illustrated in Figure 6-1. See Ref. 11, "Internet Geeks,"[1] who are creating an environment for various ecosystem collaborations.

---

[1]Internet Geeks https://www.internetgeeks.org.

© Barry Haughian 2018
B. Haughian, *Design, Launch, and Scale IoT Services*,
https://doi.org/10.1007/978-1-4842-3712-0_6

ECO System

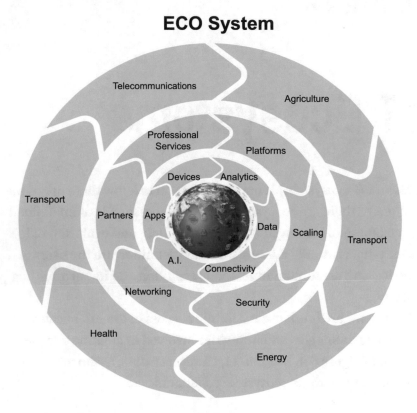

Figure 6-1. *IoT ecosystem contributors*

I was involved in an interesting discussion with a Head of the IoT
from one of my competitors who questioned why I believed ecosystems
were fundamental for the success of IoT. I was advocating an ecosystem with
collaborations were necessary to support growth. He had the view it wasn't
necessary, his company could provide all the components and services;
therefore, collaborations weren't in his plans. The truth is we were both
right. In many scenarios, the service owner can still be successful without
creating an ecosystem. However, we are in a phase of major disruption in
many industry verticals, and the IoT services contributing to this disruption
will require ecosystems. The most successful services will be those that
can bring together players from different backgrounds, competencies, and
industries working together to create a new value proposition.

In this chapter, we will look at some examples of ecosystems and discuss how and why they should be developed.

IE Business School Industry Ecosystem Challenge

I was presented with a great opportunity to evolve our ecosystem plans via the International Business School in Madrid. The Head of the MBA program, Erik Schile, invited Ericsson to participate in the MBA program's Corporate Challenge. The MBA program brings the students on a business journey by developing their knowledge and skills and promoting thought leadership. During the course, the students are offered the opportunity to apply these skills by working with multi-nationals such as Ericsson. Figure 6-2 shows the students at the kick-off event where we defined the objectives for their MBA module called the IE Business School Impact Lab.

Figure 6-2. *Ecosystem challenge*

The challenge we set was this: "How might we help Ericsson create, activate, grow, maintain, and retain a powerful set of ecosystems for IoT services in one year's time?"

This was an excellent opportunity to continue to develop and test our IoT ecosystem plans, working with business executives from 45 nationalities and diverse business backgrounds. The MBA program offered a ready-made ecosystem where we could mentor (and learn from) the students as they developed IoT ecosystem ideas.

The students were divided into groups, each working with an industry of their choice in which they had to devise an executable plan for Ericsson to create an IoT ecosystem. We defined the outcome as following: "This challenge is an actionable strategy and plan for short-term execution so that we can reach the ambitioned position." The students were encouraged to investigate and experiment with existing strategies before tackling the challenge of developing their plan. They were open to make their own assumptions when creating the plan and expected to pitch it to the assessment team in an innovative manner. In innovation, no idea is a bad idea!

We defined the following criteria for assessing the results as these were the parameters we considered key for developing our ecosystem strategy. These are common challenges that will be relevant for all ecosystem development plans irrespective of the industry vertical.

- Implementation cost

- Scalability and sustainability

- Is the plan realistic? How easy is it to implement?

- How can it be presented to stakeholders?

The analysis of existing ecosystems showed that the most successful had one of the following ecosystem enablers:

- Offer a product/service for free such as Android

- Offer a game-changing product for the industry such as iPhone

- Offer a new sales channel such as the Google Playstore

Each enabler presents unique challenges but exhibits how the successful creation of an ecosystem (via a service or product) can position the owner in a strong market position. Unfortunately, these examples may not be relevant for many services, and their implementation alone may not be sufficient for the creation of an ecosystem. Does every new IoT service expect to have the success of the Google Playstore or iPhone? Does creating a great service guarantee success without a marketing plan to gain exposure? Offering a product or service free of charge to attract players to an ecosystem is an expensive exercise and may not be possible for many IoT companies. The creation of an ecosystem isn't the end goal, but it improves the chances of a successful IoT service. Therefore, the ecosystem development plan will have to balance the cost with the benefits accrued.

The industry verticals selected by the students were quite varied and included government, tourism, transport, farming, recycling, and telecommunications (which curiously wasn't one of the final proposals). The analysis focused on the opportunities for Ericsson to enter these verticals with the following ecosystem enablers:

- Set up labs within existing local organizations to foster innovation

- Partnerships with existing universities (future business leaders)

- One-off global event to promote the company within the IoT space

- Validate industry-specific IoT ecosystems (targeted audiences)

- Marketplace to attract industry-specific companies

All but the first of these could be relevant for a small company launching an IoT service. Business labs already exist in many multinationals; therefore, the establishment and maintenance would be possible for Ericsson but would prove too costly for smaller companies. Collaboration with universities increases exposure as many of the graduates will work for companies that could become collaborators, partners, or clients in the future (a very long-term strategy). Global events can be key for success; they should not be used for pure sales as they can offer many other opportunities for ecosystem creation. The validation of specific ecosystems was quite a surprise to me; I had always assumed the creation of an ecosystem would imply throwing a wide net. However, it does make sense to have a strategy to focus on targeted groups and spread the net wider as the service grows.

The winners presented an agriculture ecosystem leveraging Ericsson's existing innovation centers to attract customers with demos and training for staff and customers. Ericsson's global reach benefitted customers by having a central reference point for IoT agricultural services to be marketed globally. Existing partnerships with universities would enable the development of cutting-edge IoT farming services, reducing the time to market.

In my feedback, I suggested the winning plan seemed to be long-term, and it needed to be coupled with a few quick wins employed in a short-term approach. I concluded that collaboration with industry-specific companies would be required for a company such as Ericsson to gain credibility quickly, and this approach will be relevant for many new IoT services.

Transportation Ecosystem

While developing IoT services, I have been approached with many requests for POCs, demos, and collaborations. These came from distinct industries and can demonstrate the benefits of an ecosystem approach. The following example was developed by a member of the sales team as a result of discussions with companies on three different continents.

- *Company A*: An airport requested to connect their motion devices to our IoT platform. The service they were planning was to track the flow of passengers through the airport. This would permit rental of retail space to be based on the number of travelers passing by the shops.

- *Company B*: A connected transport cloud company requested an AaS model for deploying their devices and software for a bus transportation company. Their device enabled an automatic payment and location positioning service.

- *Company C*: A logistics company requested storage of data for advanced analytics capabilities to implement intelligent scheduling of resources.

- *Company D*: A transport company requested a POC for a messaging service for a connected vehicle solution.

The service that could be developed by combining these distinct requests is related to revenue assurance for a bus company.

Consider the following scenario:

- Commuters board a bus using an automatic payment system and are registered by the motion detection service.

- The payment service reports that 20 payments have been received, but 30 passengers have boarded the bus.

- The messaging service enables a message to be sent to the driver advising that some passengers may have boarded without paying.

- The messaging service enables a message to be sent to a bus inspector with location data to board at next the bus top.

- The bus inspector coordinates with the driver to check the passengers at the next available stop.

- The analytics service enables the inspector to assess which dates/times/routes have the most fraud through historical data.

The ecosystem approach allowed the development of assets that could be reused in other industry verticals. This increased their value and facilitated the rapid implementation of a new service.

It has been suggested to me that invention not only consists of creating new products but increasingly consists of combining existing products and services to be used in a new manner to invent something new. This will become a reality in the IoT revolution.

Innovation with Ecosystem Partners

Ecosystems are great for fostering innovation, which will be key for many IoT services to realize their full potential.

Innovation doesn't necessarily mean creating a new IoT service. It can be related to many aspects within an IoT service, for example, innovating to optimize operational activities. Involving engineers who are performing the day-to-day operational tasks and who understand many quick wins can create innovative ideas that reduce cost and complexity for services. I often use workshops and sponsor innovation competitions with ecosystem collaborators to promote innovation.

For example, I wanted to expand our IoT energy services portfolio, and the approach I used was to sponsor a competition with an energy partner. I believed my organization didn't have enough competence in this sector, so I asked an ecosystem partner for help. I requested the opportunity to sponsor a competition in their organization to propose new IoT energy services related to consumer services. We ended up with two winners. The first suggested a smart city automated energy prioritization service in the case of blackouts. It would prioritize emergency services and key buildings, ensuring power was maintained until normal service resumed. The second winner suggested an IoT service related to home energy efficiency. I couldn't see a clear business case for this and didn't propose it for a road map item. However, their unique presentation method was adopted by our sales teams for other services. Innovation can come in many forms.

Note that careful consideration needs to be given to IPR when collaborating with external organizations and sponsoring events such as innovation competitions. If an idea does not come from the sponsor, it needs to be clearly defined who has IPR ownership and if it can be implemented without restrictions.

Conclusion

The creation and management of an IoT ecosystem should not be taken for granted. It needs to be planned, priced, and executed as part of the business strategy. Every IoT service has the potential of creating an ecosystem, and we are likely to see many ecosystems created with partnerships between newly cooperating industries, IoT suppliers, and service users. Each ecosystem will have its unique challenges to develop and grow, but the common factors described earlier should be relevant for most and will be key for many to be successful. See Ref. 12, "Internet of Things Council Eco-system," and Ref. 13, "IEEE Internet of Things."[2, 3]

---

[2]Internet of Things Council Eco-system https://www.theinternetofthings.eu/.
[3]IEEE Internet of Things iot.ieee.org.

CHAPTER 7

IoT Enablers

This chapter covers IoT enablers, these are the companies offering services to support the development of IoT services.

Service Providers

No IoT book would be complete without mentioning some of the major IoT players. In this chapter, we will take a brief look at some of the major IoT providers (*enablers*). They are a key part of the IoT revolution as they facilitate the creation of the IoT services by offering IoT platforms, tools, and professional services. These platforms and services decrease complexity and cost, reducing the time to market and enable many of the innovative IoT services to become viable businesses.

It can be quite a challenge for service owners to select the most suitable IoT business enabler, and often they will use more than one. The analysis required is supported by a wealth of material on the Internet, but it can often be contradictory, constantly changing, or difficult to decipher. Usually, the first consideration is the cost, but the service owner should take the time to filter out the criteria that is relevant for their unique service before drawing any conclusions. The best approach is to define the relevant assessment criteria before investigating the service enabler options rather than trying to assess the wide array of platforms (and services). For example,

© Barry Haughian 2018
B. Haughian, *Design, Launch, and Scale IoT Services*,
https://doi.org/10.1007/978-1-4842-3712-0_7

if billing support isn't required, remove it from the equation and simplify the analysis. Table 7-1 gives an overview of the most common criteria that should be used for assessing IoT enablers. For further reading see Ref. 14, "Comparing Platforms to Add Internet of Things Capabilities to Products."[1]

Table 7-1. *Overview of Assessing IoT Enablers*

Service portfolio	Is all the required functionality available from one provider? A "one-stop shop" can simplify the management of IoT services, and this can be critical for smaller service providers. This isn't an issue for many of the bigger services, and they often use more than one provider when the service has scaled (introducing competition between suppliers).
Ease of use	Does the platform require complex programming skills or contain complex platform-specific tools?
Application layer	What tools are available to implement the service access functionality (in other words, portals, dashboards, and so on)?
Data management	How is the IoT data retrieved from the devices stored, and how easy is it to access and manipulate?
Device management	IoT services require functionality to reduce complexity for managing and accessing devices as volumes grow. What tools are available?
Professional services	What services are available to support the IoT service in terms of technology and growth?

(*continued*)

---

[1]Comparing Platforms to Add Internet of Things Capabilities to Products www.engineering.com.

Table 7-1. (*continued*)

Security	What level of security is provided? How is access and identity management implemented? How are devices made secure, and what level of data encryption is available? Are higher security features available for highly regulated or government-related IoT services?
Compatibility	Apart from supporting the current devices, what other protocols may be required as the service evolves? Can an IoT service be integrated with other components from other providers?

Many of the major IoT enablers are also providing IaaS, PaaS, SaaS, or a combination of them. The trend suggests that the major players will continue to expand their portfolios to include components required by most IoT services. This reduces complexity, but the downside is that once a service is deployed, it may become increasingly difficult to change platform (although platforms such as ThingWorx are now compatible with AWS, Azure, and so on). Many IoT service owners only consider the initial cost and technical requirements, but they should also be assessed on their capability to support growth and their business support functions. In general, the major IoT providers all have global deployment capabilities and can support business growth, but the costs can vary significantly.

I will give a brief overview of some of the major IoT providers. There are obvious omissions such as Google, Cisco, Ayla, and more, but I have included only a few for illustration purposes. I will give an overview of AWS, IBM and Azure (enablers from a cloud service background), Ericsson, Huawei (from a connectivity perspective), and finally ThingWorx (from an application enablement background).

Note   The industry vertical–specific providers (such as Siemens and GE for manufacturing) should be analyzed to assess suitability within each sector.

I should point out that none of these is endorsed over others, and it is important that service owners perform their own investigation for their specific business needs.

AWS

AWS started with cloud and infrastructure as a service and has become one of the major leaders of IoT. It provides a comprehensive range of services that reduce the complexity required to create and commercialize IoT services. Its core IoT service allows devices and gateways to be connected to rule engines in an elastic, scalable manner. The device "shadow" models the physical device, and the data from the device can be reused easily, in other words, routed to the other Amazon services such Kinesis, DynamoDB, Lambda, S3, and Amazon ML. The cost of Amazon services needs to be calculated carefully as the range of payment possibilities is quite extensive due to the wide range of services on offer. Fortunately, they provide a calculator to simplify this task.

AWS adds professional services to the platform capabilities for enterprises to assist in the development of IoT services in terms of architecture and business.

These are the key IoT-related features:

- *AWS IoT Core*: Provides the capability to securely connect devices to the cloud and other devices

- AWS *IoT Device*: Offers the capability to register, manage, and monitor IoT devices.

- *AWS IoT Analytics*: Offers tools to automate data analysis from IoT devices with reporting capabilities

- *Greengrass*: Facilitates local deployment of IoT services including Lambda and ML capabilities

- *Amazon ML*: Offers machine learning APIs for advanced IoT functions

- *Kinesis* : Offers data streaming and processing capabilities

- *Cloudwatch*: Offers monitoring tools for applications, devices, databases, and so on

- *AWS Developer*: Offers a wide range of tools supporting open source development

Microsoft IoT Azure

Microsoft is another leading player with a full array of IaaS and PaaS services, allowing rapid development of IoT services. It offers a wide range of tools that are scalable and can be easily integrated with other software and hardware. As with other easily IoT platform service providers, it charges on a pay-as-you-grow model, in other words, based on the number of messages/data sent/received. This is a model that lends itself well to IoT AaS. As with most platforms, it offers SDKs that are both open source and for the Windows platform, and it has a wide range of partners with certified devices and starter kits.

It provides extensive support with professional services to assist with the development of IoT services.

Here are the key IoT-related features:

- *IoT HUB*: Enables the connection and management of devices with bidirectional data flow including device simulation and edge computing

- *IoT Azure Central*: Enables the creation of IoT applications with connected devices that offers central monitoring with device rules

- *IoT Solution*: Provides solutions that can be used as templates for accelerating IoT service development

- *IoT Edge*: Permits Azure services (such as AI and analytics) to be deployed locally

- *Event HUB*: Enables the management of events and data received from devices including triggering

- *Machine Learning*: Offers cloud-based cognitive API services

- *Analytics*: Provides a wide range of analytics services including real-time analysis, big data, and machine learning functions

- *Developer*: Offers a Visual Studio developer environment supporting many open source SDKs, languages, and environments

Huawei

Huawei provides a cloud service with PaaS through IoT partnerships and has developed many IoT services. Currently it offers IoT capabilities through its products by exposing APIs, with an open ecosystem built on IoT, cloud computing, and big data technology. The IoT Connection Management Platform contains a lot of the functionality required by

IoT services. It provides a remote lab for developing and testing IoT services after entering into a partnership agreement.

The portfolio includes the following:

- *OceanConnect*: Provides a developer environment with APIs and IoT applications, simplifying device access, and network connection management.

- *EC-IoT*: It implements Huawei edge computing service via an Agile controller and gateway

- *Communication*: IoT connection platform providing E2E communication capabilities

PTC/ThingWorx

This is an IoT platform providing capabilities to connect, build, manage, analyze, and launch new IoT services. It offers rapid application development tools that can monitor, manage, and control connected devices. It allows bidirectional support for remote data collection, providing secure connectivity between devices. It also provides device/sensor management/integration with third-party systems (including Amazon and Azure IoT platforms). In its portfolio it offers supporting tools such as a developer portal, a marketplace, and services such as AR and VR.

The current portfolio includes the following:

- *Foundation*: Provides rapid application development tools for connected devices with an Application Environment Platform (AEP), connection services, edge capabilities, and device/data management

- *IoT Manager*: Provides asset, event, and workflow management tools that can assist operational management activities

- *Analytics*: Provides an analytics tool that includes predictive capabilities to enable automation of analytics with edge capabilities

- *Studio*: Provides advanced and easy to use AR functionality including capabilities for building and publishing AR applications

- *Manufacturing*: Provides ThingWorx manufacturing apps, which are a set of role-based starter apps built on the IoT platform

IBM

IBM is typically an IaaS provider, but it is moving up the stack with services such as data and device management, analytics, and security. Its main product is Watson, which allows users to define devices, receive, and analyze data. It is constantly increasing the portfolio of Watson, which has been traditionally considered an AI platform. It now includes a lot more IoT-related functionality. It also offers Bluemix, a powerful suite of tools offering the ability to create IoT applications by providing SDKs and open APIs.

The current portfolio includes the following:

- *Watson IoT*: Provides a cloud-based connectivity service for connecting and managing IoT devices. It offers the ability to manage and integrate IoT device data, and incorporates blockchain technology to increase security

- *Analytics*: Provides a wide range of advanced analytics capabilities combined with advanced machine learning capabilities

- *Developer*: Provides a cloud-based suite of platform tools to develop IoT services and manage devices

- *IoT Edge*: Provides the possibility to deploy AI and analytics on edge devices

Ericsson

Ericsson entered the IoT space with the acquisition of the Device Connection Platform, providing connectivity management services. It has been evolving its offering with platforms such as the IoT Accelerator that offer additional IoT services such as data and device management and so on.

The current portfolio includes the following:

- *Connectivity*: Provides enterprises with the ability to manage the connectivity of their devices

- *Orchestration*: Provides device and data management features, including data modeling

- *Integration*: Provides an automation framework that offers functionality for analytics processing, data storage, a monetization engine, security, and so on

- *IoT Marketplace*: Enables an enterprise's administration capabilities, developer and partner onboarding, API exposure, and a white-label portal to develop ecosystems

IoT Enablers: Professional Services

The IoT revolution has arrived partly because the complexity of producing IoT services has decreased dramatically. IoT services that address specific use cases are easier to create because of advances in technology, manufacturing, and communication. However, not everything can be automated, and there is still a need for professional services to complement the advances in technology.

Many of the IoT enablers offer horizontal platforms (in other words, they support multiple vertical industries) complemented with professional services. Often, they can provide specialized knowledge leveraging ecosystems and experience from solutions developed on their platforms.

The importance of professional services can be illustrated by my discussions with a manufacturing plant that wanted to perform a digital transformation to increase productivity and reduce costs. They were in the procurement process and investigating whether implementing services on an IoT platform could benefit their business. I presented our IoT platform explaining the usual services such as device management, data management, and analytics services. Before everyone fell asleep, I was asked, "There are numerous platforms available; what makes your platform the one they should select?" My honest was answer was that there were better platforms that could serve a lot of their use cases. However, we could provide the professional support services that were required to realize the full transformation. It couldn't be done with technology alone. We could offer consulting for process optimization, migration, transformation, and an operations center to support field services. The differentiator for many IoT enablers will not always be the IoT services available. It will be the additional professional services on offer to support the business objectives such as global expansion, digital transformation, optimization, and cost reduction.

Figure 7-1 illustrates the most common services that are offered by IoT enablers. It can be useful to avail of these services during the development of new IoT services or additional features. The cost of each cannot be calculated before some analysis; therefore, they are often charged using hourly or daily rates (time and material). Although these do not require industry-specific knowledge, it can be a big advantage if the IoT enabler has already developed solutions in the same industry vertical and can provide industry-specific knowledge.

PROFESSIONAL SERVICES	
PRE-SALES SUPPORT	Design sales material and participate in sales meetings
TRANSITIONAL MANAGEMENT	Support customer subsequent to service launch
CUSTOMIZED REPORTING	Create specific customer reports
BUSINESS CONSULTING	Consultation services to improve business/service performance
DEVICE AND APP VERIFICATION	Verifying new devices and applications
DATA MIGRATION	Migration of existing customer base to the service
APP. DEVELOPMENT & MAINTENANCE	Customer specific application development and maintenance
OPERATION AND FIELD SERVICES	Implement a service desk with workforce management
SYSTEMS INTEGRATION	Integration services towards other systems

Figure 7-1. *IoT professional services*

IoT service owners can request these services from IoT enablers, but they should also consider offering these professional services to their customers as they can be a useful additional revenue stream.

Presales Support

IoT concepts (like AaS business models) and services are new to many industry verticals. This introduces challenges for service owners to communicate their sales pitch during presales discussions with potential customers. If the service owner does not have the sufficient experience or competence, contracting sales support can be a useful solution. It should be considered at service launch as it may prove to be a short-term solution to develop quality sales material and avail of the broader knowledge in the IoT space.

Activities required by presales support typically include the following:

- Training sales and marketing staff to develop the value proposition

- Creating and developing sales presentations

- Supporting the sales organization from a technical and business perspective

- Capturing new service requirements to be delivered to service managers based on customer feedback

Transition Management

Transition management is normally carried out by an operational consultant who facilitates the smooth introduction of new IoT services. They assist the customer organizations to fully understand the new service and how to achieve maximum benefit from its introduction.

The transitional manager aims to do the following:

- Support customer organizations in transitioning from the delivery project to a commercial operational setup.

- Ensure the customer representatives are familiar with service documentation and understand the support processes/procedures.

- Act as an SPOC to address post-deployment-related questions.

- Provide support and mentoring to the customer managers who are responsible for the service when the transition period expires. It can be useful for customers to appoint a "shadow" for the transitional manager during the transition period.

- Identify areas of improvement within the customer's organization, regarding processes and interactions between the customer and service owner.

Customized Reporting

Typically, the service description outlines a set of standard reports that are accessible through a service portal. However, service providers should expect to receive customized reporting requests based on a customer's unique business requirements. Offering a professional service to develop reports in a specific format or require a change to the availability of reports can be a useful additional revenue stream. The cost of customized reports should be calculated as a combination of the initial development costs, the recurring delivery costs, and the lifecycle management of the report. Note that automation is key to controlling operational costs related to the recurring delivery of customized reporting.

Business Consulting

The transitional management service may lead to the customer requesting business consulting to provide advisory services. This service provides the customers with analysis on all aspects of their business to improve performance, achieve competitive advantage, and ultimately increase the success of the service. It is most beneficial when the consultant can provide specialist domain knowledge and market insights.

It requires a broad understanding of the IoT service landscape in terms of business, financial, IT, and network challenges. The consultant can leverage execution experience from other customers to propose recommendations related to service operations, marketing, sales, road map features, and so on.

Device and Application Verification

Device and application verification is required to ensure that new device types and applications comply with service limitations (usually related to technical or capacity constraints).

The tests typically include compatibility verification for signaling, data transfer, and capacity measurements. More advanced tests may include device security checks or battery consumption. If possible, these tests should be automated in a lab environment, but it can be more cost effective to give customers access to the lab to perform the tests under supervision.

The importance of this can be illustrated by a catastrophic chain of events when a customer introduced a new device without performing mandatory acceptance tests. The device crashed the service by sending unrecognizable messages (due to an incompatible format). This resulted in repeated signaling attempts from the device (as no acknowledgment message was received) Finally, the service experienced signaling congestion on the communication layer, and certified devices were unable to send messages, causing a complete service outage. The lesson to be learned is that all changes to the service should be verified before being introduced to the live environment. Executing a device application and service can be a useful tool to avoid these issues.

Data Migration

Data migration usually consists of a project to transfer the existing customer data from a legacy service to the new IoT service system components. In its most basic form, it can be the transfer of a database, but this too can become a complex operation. It requires significant testing with a fallback plan in place in case of issues. The process should be offered in a very service-oriented method, implying that the customer does not know or get involved in the complexities of the migration. The cost can be significant if automated tools are not available for transforming data structures; therefore, a prestudy may be required to ensure its feasibility and cost-effectiveness.

Application Development and Maintenance

Customers often require outsourcing of software development and maintenance as they do not have the capacity or competence to develop and maintain software in a cost-effective manner. The service is usually performed by engineers who are competent with the application layer of the IoT stack and its interaction with middle-layer components. The requests may consist of a new application that communicates with existing service modules or feature add-ons. The development of the service or add-ons will be a one-off cost, but service providers should also consider the maintenance as a recurring cost.

Operations Service Desk and Field Services

Customers or service owners may request the outsourcing of service desk operational activities if there isn't enough scale or revenue being generated to merit its creation in the operations organization. Scale is required to be cost effective, and this can be a challenge for newly launched services.

Typically, a service desk will perform the following activities:

- Register issues or service requests

- Evaluate information received and complement if necessary

- Solve the customer problem directly or escalate to the appropriate organization

- Monitor the progress of the fault or service request

- Manage the supporting processes for fault resolution, including change management together with the external service providers

The service desk connects to the field services organization by registering and managing requests that require actions by field service engineers. The field services activities are required if engineers cannot complete activities remotely, such as if an engineer must travel to replace a remotely located faulty device. Outsourcing of field operations is most cost-effective if the deployment of the service/devices is over a wide geographical area or in the early phases of service launch. If the device volumes haven't reached critical mass, it may not be efficient to have engineers dedicated to field operations.

Most field service operation organizations implement workforce management via an enterprise service bus (see Chapter 3). It reduces opex by automating business processes and providing the intelligent scheduling of activities to improve the efficiency of the field operations. For example, if a customer registers a request, it automatically initiates the scheduling of a work order that is sent to a field engineer planning their daily/weekly activities. Workforce management can also provide track and trace capabilities by storing information regarding all service requests and can provide valuable analytical information to improve efficiency.

Systems Integration

IoT services should have clear definitions, clear interfaces, and plan for scaling. The implications of this are that the service should not require complex system integration activities. However, this may not be the case when the customer has business-critical legacy systems and the service provider should consider integrations as an additional chargeable service. System integration needs to be carefully scoped and priced to ensure it fits into the business, technical, and operational models of the service. I have rejected many service integration requests from customers as they required modification to service components and there was little chance of reuse. System integration activities are normally carried out by DevOps engineers, and complex projects can put considerable pressure on that organization. The subsequent maintenance of the service also needs to be planned and priced on a time and material basis.

CHAPTER 8

IoT Industries

The Internet revolution has resulted in a major disruption for many industries. It started with the development of the World Wide Web (the 1990s) and the evolved with the mobile Internet (the 2000s), forcing many to rethink their business models and embrace this disruptive technology. We are now heading to the third and potentially most disruptive phase of the Internet revolution—the Internet of Things. Objects from the real world will be modeled in the virtual world and connected via the Internet. This will result in humans and devices being connected at any time and from any place, and the implications are impossible to predict.

Figure 8-1 (see Ref. 15, "Forecasts Worldwide Spending on the Internet of Things to Reach $772 Billion in 2018"[1]) illustrates that IoT revenues are so big that there are countless opportunities for new services. There are opportunities in almost all industry verticals, with just 1 percent of the manufacturing vertical estimated to be $1.89 billion.

---

[1]Forecasts Worldwide Spending on the Internet of Things to Reach $772 Billion in 2018. IDC https://www.idc.com.

© Barry Haughian 2018
B. Haughian, *Design, Launch, and Scale IoT Services*,
https://doi.org/10.1007/978-1-4842-3712-0_8

Industry	Use Case	Revenue in Billions
Cross Industry	Connected vehicles and smart buildings	92
Consumer	Smart home, including home automation, security, and smart appliances	62
Manufacturing	Support manufacturing operations and production asset management	189
Utilities	Smart grids for electricity, gas, and water	73
Transportation	Freight monitoring, followed by fleet management	85

Figure 8-1. *IoT industries (source: IDC Research 2018)*

In this section, I will discuss some of the industry sectors and business opportunities available. The disruption to each industry vertical is unique and needs to be considered independently to understand the opportunities.

To be able to take advantage of the opportunities created by the IoT revolution, industry experts do not have to be experts in IoT. The reverse also applies, and cooperation will provide the greatest success. I usually start my IoT customer engagements by explaining that IoT can open new opportunities and business streams previously not available. I am not an expert in any specific industry vertical, but I can incorporate IoT into their business. In many cases, this will remove the business, operational and technology challenges permitting the customer to concentrate on their core business.

An example of this is illustrated by a major train company that requested an investigation to propose IoT solutions that could improve their customer experience and reduce costs. We had the preconceived idea that the key improvements would relate to the automation and scheduling of their train services to optimize fuel consumption or provide services to their end customers. After several workshops, we realized that the major issue they needed to solve was related to their operations organization. They needed an efficient IoT service to optimize their enormous operations workforce that maintained the network of railway tracks. This IoT service would require the deployment of thousands of sensors on railway tracks that could report faults to a central IoT system. It would classify the fault and automate workforce management for the maintenance engineers optimizing their workload and reduce costs.

I was questioned, "Could this be classified as an IoT service?" I responded that it didn't matter if we called it IoT, but it ticked all my boxes. The service we defined consisted of large volumes of devices/sensors deployed and sending data over the Internet to solve a problem. The result allowed the company to improve operations, reduce costs, and focus on their core business: the train service.

Note that this same service could be repeated for other transport scenarios by simply modifying the upper layer of the IoT stack.

Industry Disruption

Internet users are estimated to grow to 6.5 billion in 2020, and the number of sensors is projected to grow to more than 50 billion in 2020. Whether we believe these numbers doesn't really matter; it seems there will be a lot more devices than people using the Internet. This doesn't necessarily imply a disruption for industries, but there are few factors that are contributing to the belief that we are on the cusp of something big.

The cost of implementing IoT services is reducing drastically. New tools are available to reduce the complexity (and cost) required to develop the services. The cost of producing hardware falls year after year as the capacity increases. This has resulted in a much broader range of industries being able to take advantage of the IoT revolution. The ability to offer services in a "pay-as-you-grow" model allows many second and third-tier companies to enter the IoT space. It has also resulted in a lot more opportunities for startups as it offers the possibility for companies with small investments to offer services within industry verticals that would have been previously out of reach. We can now see examples in the energy sector where IoT services are being offered that analyze energy consumption and take optimizing actions based on the results. This would have been unthinkable for a startup ten years ago.

Another positive disruption is that non-cooperating industries have the possibility to collaborate and offer new or improved services. If the IoT revolution is successful, it will open the possibility for new innovative businesses to create ecosystems that ultimately disrupt all industries. For example, traditional telecoms companies are moving into different sectors, hiring consultants to develop offerings in verticals that they previously didn't consider as part of their business plans.

Almost all industry verticals are impacted, but I have selected just a few to illustrate the challenges and business opportunities available in each sector. For further reading on IoT verticals, see Ref. 16, "IoT Business News," and Ref. 17, "RFID Journal."[2, 3]

Smart City

The term *smart city* is overused, and I have never been in a discussion where we reached a common definition. Figure 8-2 illustrates many of the services associated with smart cities. Some of these are available today, but most have a long evolution ahead of them.

---

[2]IoT Business News https://iotbusinessnews.com.
[3]RFID Journal http://www.rfidjournal.com/internet-of-things.

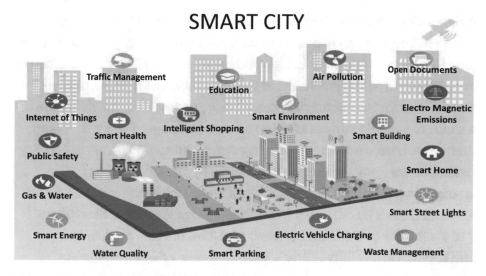

Figure 8-2. *Smart city services*

The following definition is generic but encompasses most of the aspects generally associated with smart cities: a smart city is an urban development vision to integrate information and communication technology (ICT) and Internet of Things technology in a secure fashion to manage a city's assets.

The hype surrounding smart cities is considerable, and there are many diverse services being labeled as smart city offerings. Therefore, it can be beneficial for many IoT services to be described as smart city offerings to take advantage of the hype.

Often, smart cities are driven by government bodies (either central, regional, or city) that want to provide a better service to the citizens or increase efficiency in public services. Many public bodies employ independent bodies to oversee the tendering process for smart city contracts to ensure transparency and equal competition. This can have the knock-on effect of introducing long sales cycles for IoT service companies, and this needs to be considered in the sales process for public tenders.

As the smart city concept becomes more widespread, the definition of a smart city should consolidate into a common range of services. Already there have been some attempts to standardize the work related to smart cities. For example, the European Union in its funding for smart cities is suggesting compatibility with FIWARE as the reference architecture. FIWARE defines its mission as, "The objective of FIWARE is to facilitate a cost-effective creation and delivery of Future Internet applications and services in a variety of areas, including smart cities, sustainable transport, logistics, renewable energy, and environmental sustainability." Compatibility with this architecture may prove useful for many services.

One aspect that most smart city deployments have in common is that there will be an incremental approach to their implementation. Many cities have started by implementing a transport service and continue by adding other services. The diversity in smart cities can be illustrated by a few smart city examples where each city has defined an initial use case that they want to have solved and describe it is as a smart city service.

- *Spain smart city*: Focused on tourism via the creation of an ecosystem that connects devices to travelers to improve the tourism experience. The devices transmit data to be used by tourists free of charge in apps and smart devices.

- *Romania smart city*: Focused on residents, improving their day-to-day quality of life by implementing a free smart parking service to reduce city congestion.

- *Netherlands smart city*: Focused on reducing CO_2 emissions by implementing intelligent traffic systems to reduce traffic congestion. Vehicles and traffic lights communicate by advising when lights are about to change color, allowing drivers to optimize their velocity.

- *United States smart city*: Focused on controlling the energy consumption required by the state. A smart street lighting service is the first of many new IoT services to reduce energy consumption.

In general, these services have one thing in common; they are free for residents (or users) of the smart city. The implication is that any potential service developed under a smart city umbrella may have to incorporate this business model. This does not imply that there isn't a successful growable revenue stream for the service provider. They will be paid by the government body, but they can also investigate additional business streams by creating smart city ecosystems. For example, if residents are using a smart city app, there may be additional revenue opportunities for advertising to be sold. It should be noted that government contracts can often be quite complex, and the service provider should ensure that the T&C allow for the possibility to sell additional services.

The city of Santander in Spain is a good example of the implementation of a smart city where they are attempting to create an ecosystem powered by IoT service providers. They are promoting innovation by providing a central location to offer and promote IoT services that can become part of their smart city evolution.

The key to successful smart cities will be to create an ecosystem of companies that are exposing their data to be reused in other use cases. This will promote innovation and the development of new use cases. In most cases, the creation of the ecosystem will include a central portal that contains the services and resources for the future development and promotion of innovative use cases.

Smart Home

I was asked to advise a number of IoT startup companies on their smart home service proposals. In preparation, I presented the service specifications to my IoT management team, and after a heated debate we concluded that most of the ideas wouldn't be successful. We concluded that many of the services faced tough competition from similar services that were already commercially available. Smart home services are becoming a very congested space, with many startups targeting this vertical. Figure 8-3 highlights some of the most common use cases.

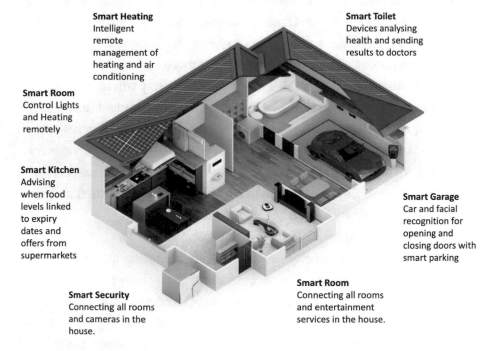

Smart Heating
Intelligent remote management of heating and air conditioning

Smart Toilet
Devices analysing health and sending results to doctors

Smart Room
Control Lights and Heating remotely

Smart Kitchen
Advising when food levels linked to expiry dates and offers from supermarkets

Smart Garage
Car and facial recognition for opening and closing doors with smart parking

Smart Security
Connecting all rooms and cameras in the house.

Smart Room
Connecting all rooms and entertainment services in the house.

Figure 8-3. *Smart homes*

The main challenges for smart home services will be the development of distribution channels, the GTM strategies, and how to monetize on the service. The services require volumes, and the challenges are how to sell to many homes and how to deploy the service in a cost-efficient manner. The solution for many will be partnerships and selling through existing retailers already offering products for homes. The service should be designed to offer the ability for installation to be performed by the homeowners. Services that do not offer this ability may have issues with scaling and maintaining margins.

Although each smart home service will have unique challenges, a common issue that should be considered a high priority is security. All commercially deployed services will require a high level of security to prevent hacking or unauthorized access to home networks. A lot of the services are deployed with cameras in homes or devices that store confidential information. The current trends suggests that smart home services will incorporate a VPN or a common security key to identify the devices and users as part of the home network. The service owner will need to ensure the devices are configured correctly and that monitoring can be performed to report unauthorized access attempts.

Home security IoT services generally provide a low-cost entry for the service provider where the device is developed specifically for the use case performing activities such as remote monitoring, remote cameras, and intelligent locks. The majority of these use the cellular connectivity, which can provide a sufficient level of security and QoS that is often a mandatory requirement. One consideration often overlooked is communication. Many of the devices will use a form of low-range connectivity communicating with a central hub, but this connection may not have sufficient QoS. In scenarios where you cannot guarantee QoS measures must be taken to mitigate against failure. For example, if a sensor is not responding, the service must have the ability to detect the failure and recommend the appropriate action such as informing the homeowner that they should replace a battery.

There are many established home security service companies offering home monitoring services from a central security operations center (SOC). They are usually deployed with an AaS business model charging an installation fee and monthly subscriptions. New to the market are the systems that are installed by home owners, and monitoring is performed directly on their mobile phones (outsourcing operations to the home owner). This offers new opportunities to enter this lucrative market, and we can expect many of these services to follow the AaS model as it allows the investment to increase with sales. As discussed in Chapter 9, it creates a recurring revenue model and usually offers a closer customer relationship with an increased opportunity for up-sales.

There are many options for connectivity that should be considered during the design of smart home services such as the sensors being connected to a central console via Wi-Fi. This puts a prerequisite on the home owner to have sufficient coverage for all the sensors and manage issues that arise because of communication interference. It moves the boundary of the service toward the homeowner by placing the connectivity performance between sensors and the gateway outside the scope of the service. This should be reflected in the SLA, and the contract should be designed in a way that it is very clear on accountability and responsibility for the service performance. Although service providers may not be contractually responsible for the communication between nodes within the home, they should still expect to provide support for customers to ensure the service experience is acceptable.

Smart metering services are becoming widespread (in smart homes) because of new regulations in many countries requiring the deployment of smart meters. They usually consist of smart meters reporting on electricity, gas, or water consumption. The ownership and deployment of the devices is usually managed by a smart metering company that includes an app to enable the homeowners to monitor meters remotely. There are still many possibilities for implementing intelligent systems toward these services through APIs. For example, an automated service can activate appliances intelligently or inform homeowners of changes to the price of electricity or gas. There are additional challenges for new players in this market as these industries are not heavily regulated in terms of technology. This lack of industry standards may result in services being required to support many meter types and protocols, increasing costs considerably as they scale.

Smart appliances are readily available, but the use cases for each service need to be analyzed from a business perspective. I have already mentioned the use case of a fridge being able to communicate with an oven. While I have yet to understand the business value or any logical use for this it is not meant to suggest that there will not be innovative solutions related the kitchens including the smart management of communicating fridges or ovens. Smart plugs and smart lights are becoming widely available, and we can expect their deployment to accelerate. The most important aspect to consider while designing smart home services will be their usability. If the service requires complex configuration, it is unlikely to be successful. The goal should be that as soon as the device is turned on, it is automatically deployed and can be managed easily through mobile devices. Many smart home appliances will avail of Wi-Fi available in most homes and should be designed with sufficient range to communicate a central hub/gateway.

Transportation

Transportation in IoT terms encompasses a wide range of IoT services that are in different stages of development. The most common consist of devices deployed in vehicles that report telematics data for analysis by analytics or other middleware software. Opportunities for new services are more likely to exist in the application and platform layers rather than the device layer or in the full IoT stack. There are many use cases already deployed, as illustrated in Figure 8-4, and these will continue to have a considerable impact in the IoT space in terms of hype and innovation.

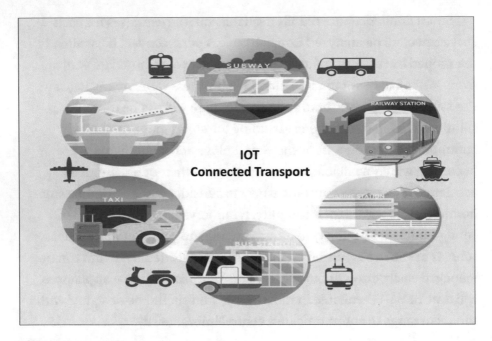

Figure 8-4. *IoT transport services*

Connected Vehicle Cloud

There are a substantial number of IoT transportation services already deployed such as autonomous driving, telematics, car infotainment, and roadside assistance. They are beginning to revolutionize our thinking regarding vehicles and the associated services. All major car manufacturers are investing in heavily connected vehicles, offering a wide range of services providing connectivity directly via devices embedded in the vehicle. The emergence of new players such as Tesla are muddying the boundaries between IT and traditional vehicle companies. The vast sums being invested by vehicle manufacturers means that it will be difficult for startups to become part of this industry vertical. They will need to carve out a niche market adding value to services already developed by the big players. Connectivity will almost certainly be cellular because of the QoS requirements and devices being mobile. Car manufacturers are forcing the reduction of connectivity costs and pushing the development of new services such as the introduction of multidomestic solutions with localized SIM capabilities. A key factor to be taken into consideration when developing a connected vehicle service is that the lifecycle of the connected device will most likely be the lifetime of the car, which is much longer than many other IoT devices.

Telematics data is currently available in most new vehicles, and it will be used by the car companies for predictive maintenance, components analysis, driver analysis, and more. At this stage, there are more questions than answers regarding the use of the data. This is a perfect environment for innovation for new IoT services. Already insurance companies are requesting access to this data to calculate insurance premiums. One of the questions to be answered that is particularly poignant for vehicle owners is, "Who has access to and owns the personal data being collected?" Security and privacy issues will be of primary concern, and there may be the possibility of owners selling the car data in the future. Regulation is far behind the innovation, and that is unlikely to change.

Connected Transport Cloud

I define connected transport services as the transport use cases that relate to the general traffic and not individual vehicles. There should be more possibilities for new services in this space than connected vehicles but with that comes more competition. There are no standard protocols for data collection as it can be provided by any number of sources, such as vehicles, traffic lights, garages, and regulatory bodies. The deployment of gateways to standardize how data is collected is likely to become fundamental for success in this space. One of the most common use cases being offered provides logistical services and real-time information for transportation companies to improve fleet efficiency. In the future, we will have the vehicles communicating in a mesh network to transmit real-time traffic data advising other vehicles in the fleet. There will be many opportunities for new services intelligently using this data.

As the devices are mobile, they may not always have the possibility to transmit because of coverage. Therefore, they should have the ability to store data and transmit it in real time or batch mode when communication is restored.

The security and legal implications of the vehicle data being transmitted will become paramount and hasn't been given the attention it deserves. Services are already providing data analysis to report on the individual performance of drivers and fleet vehicles. In the future, this will have an increasing impact on driver performance bonuses and insurance premiums, enabling transport companies to improve their margins etc.

Energy

There is considerable disruption in the energy sector because of deregulation and the introduction of new renewable energy sources. The deployment of smart metering is being rolled out across the globe with smart grid services probably not being far behind. See Ref. 18, "IoT and analytics market for utilities expected to grow to $5.1bn in 2028."[4]

During the assessment of an IoT smart metering service I was presented with a technical overview of the current service. The VP for operations illustrated a complex diagram detailing the architecture and communication flow from a hardware and software perspective. It was obvious that they would have no possibility to scale or optimize the current service because of the number different of device types, protocols and the complexity of the process flow. This is a quite common issue in the energy sector as it is not regulated and contains fragmented technology solutions. The solution to manage this complexity can be handled by the majority of IoT platforms, but with increased complexity comes increased cost. Gateways can provide part of the solution by implementing multiple

---

[4]IoT and analytics market for utilities expected to grow to $5.1bn in 2028. IoT News
https://www.iottechnews.com.

protocols to handle many device types. The IoT middleware modules such as data/device management, asset management, and enterprise bus services can be used to automate the logistical processes. IoT smart metering services will make full use of IoT platform capabilities to automate and simplify service management if they are to be efficient and profitable.

Figure 8-5 illustrates a typical smart metering service consisting of a meter that will send the data to a head-end system for consolidation before distribution to billing systems. If the meter reading is not received, there will be several automated requests to read the data. If this fails, a work order can be sent to field services requesting a manual reading. The engineer can pass near the house and take the reading remotely or request entry if the meter must be replaced. If there are multiple meter types that aren't compatible, this becomes quite a logistical challenge for the company to replace meters to ensure compliance with the SLA. This demonstrates that one of the principle challenges to be solved by many smart metering services has nothing to do with energy production. It is operational and organizational planning that can be solved by many "non-energy" IoT services. The solution will consist of data and device management, enabling intelligent asset and workforce management, all of which are available on most IoT platforms.

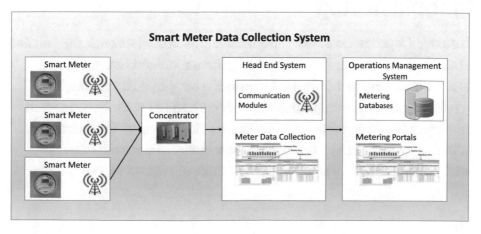

Figure 8-5. *Smart metering architecture*

If the architecture of the smart metering service does not include (enterprise) business processes and inventory management modules, it will be challenging to introduce efficiencies. Scaling will be an issue as operational costs are likely to increase in parallel with the device volumes.

Security has already been highlighted as an issue for energy providers, with hackers being able to gain access to electricity monitoring systems. Many of these incidents are reported as IoT security breaches with central IT systems being hacked. We can conclude that security is already fundamental for IoT services in this vertical, and it needs to be managed in all layers of the IoT stack (see Chapter 3 for more information).

Connectivity for meters has been implemented traditionally via PLC, and more recently cellular has become the norm. As with connected vehicle services, the lifecycle of smart metering devices can be expected to be quite long, about ten to fifteen years. Therefore, services should be designed with a view that the devices will have a long deployment period.

Manufacturing

Industry 4.0 promises to revolutionize manufacturing through the creation of smart factories. They will introduce automation and data exchange in manufacturing technologies including cyber-physical systems, IoT services, and cloud computing. Industry 4.0 and IoT are interconnected, and it will be fundamental to the success of IoT services. The production of IoT devices will require maximum automation, increased reliability, and reduced cost. The key to achieving these objectives will be via smart factories, with automation reducing human interaction from the device manufacturing process. See Ref. 19, "IoTone Accelerating the Industrial Internet of Things."[5]

Figure 8-6 shows the world's first collaborative dual arm robot that offers increased opportunities for automation in assembly manufacturing processes. Collaborative robots can work safely with humans in the manufacturing process and automate many of the mundane repeatable processes currently being executed by humans. The introduction of these robots to the manufacturing process will increase production, quality, and efficiency. The key for IoT will be how the data is extracted from the Industry 4.0 devices and used intelligently to optimise the manufacturing processes.

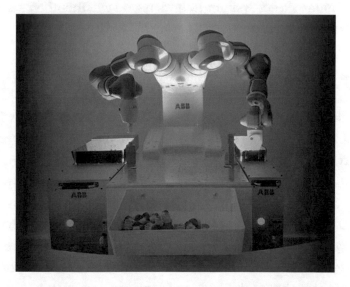

Figure 8-6. *Collaborative robot*

---

[5]"IoTone Accelerating the Industrial Internet of Things" www.iotone.com.

Although many service providers will outsource device production, there are still efficiencies that can be introduced (see Chapter 3). For example, the service owner should implement an automated process for ordering and producing devices. If a new batch of devices is required, it should trigger an automated production process that is activated when all components are available in stock. Ultimately, the goal is zero human interaction (interference). Many services allow existing customers to order new devices through a customer portal, offering increased service satisfaction and no additional operations costs as the service expands.

There are numerous opportunities for new IoT services in the manufacturing area mostly related to logistics and automation of manufacturing processes on the factory floor. Existing services should look for opportunities via ecosystems to understand whether their services can be reused in manufacturing (see Chapter 6).

Media

Many of the new revenue streams for the IoT in the media space will be associated with advertising towards the users of the deployed service. An IoT service that has a large deployment of devices to users has many opportunities for additional revenue streams because of the ecosystem created by the scale. For example, an Internet of Animals can have targeted advertising related to products to improve the current health of the animals.

Intelligent advertising has been available for quite some time, and it will be a key additional revenue stream for many IoT services. For example, an IoT service that has mobile devices deployed across a city could provide advertising related to shops and services as the devices approach specific areas.

Already we are seeing taxi services that are providing screens on the back of seats; the evolution of this service could be that once the destination is known, the taxi can implement targeted advertising from the shops on the route or at the destination.

Public Safety

The public sector is exploring how IoT can provide a higher level of service to its citizens. Often this can be considered as part of a smart city, but IoT public services generally require higher security levels than consumer-based smart city services.

This is another area where there has been a lot of hype, and it is necessary to understand the factors that enable IoT services to be used in public safety. IoT services will usually be delivered via the Internet; therefore, there may be no guaranteed quality of service, and that can be a minimum requirement for public safety services. This might sound alarming, but it can be handled if the service level agreement includes a clause to exempt the service provider if the interruption to service is outside their control. Therefore, the question needs to be asked, can IoT services be used for public safety services? The answer is yes in many scenarios. If the current service is improved by introducing IoT, then there is a value that will result in a revenue stream.

The analysis of the data can be key for public safety use cases. For example, several cities in Europe are performing trials with emergency services. If a call is received by an emergency service, they can be advised of the best route to reach their destination. More advanced trials route the emergency service, with traffic lights being activated to remain green for the emergency service route.

IoT services in disaster zones might not seem so obvious as it is likely the Internet and infrastructure will be down if there is a disaster. However, drone technology can provide radio coverage as a backup for communications. There will be many innovative services that can improve public safety, as illustrated in Figure 8-7. The key message is that care must be taken that they are used in the correct context with the correct contractual T&C.

Figure 8-7. *IoT public safety use cases*

Health

The possibilities for IoT health services are endless; the most common are services such as remote patient monitoring or remote diagnosis. Almost every phone or smart wristband can monitor our health, which can become part of much bigger IoT services. One aspect that is still in its infancy is that of smart hospitals, where the IoT services are supporting the overall management of the hospitals. The IoT services will optimize and track hospital resources as with any smart building, increasing efficiency and reducing cost. We are likely to see 5G offering new possibilities of real-time medical services that can be deployed in hospitals or for in-home healthcare services.

The challenge for many services will be QoS, which is difficult for many services to guarantee (chemical analysis sensors can have a limited lifetime and questionable reliability). Remote patient monitoring has been implemented in many countries, and most would agree that while there are no 100 percent guarantees with the service, the patient is better off with it than without it. The key is to implement processes that take clear corrective actions in cases of service interruption such as device or communication failure. There also must be an agreement between the service provider and service receiver in case of failure. For example, many devices are monitoring the health of patients to report back data for automatic analysis. In the future if the device or communication fails to report back data the patient should have a backup procedure available. An alarm can be sent to advise the patient to go to a hospital to have manual readings performed or to have the device replaced.

In this chapter, we have seen some of the major industry verticals that are impacted by the IoT. The opportunities are endless, and each IoT service will have to find its niche market opportunity within the vertical. I usually suggest "no idea is a bad idea," but the key message here is that the service should have the ability to adapt quickly as the service evolves and industry specific market conditions change.

CHAPTER 9

Business Model

This chapter covers the fundamentals of an AaS business model explaining why it is suitable for IoT services. It concludes by outlining many key factors that are present in successful IoT services and many of the issues the cause IoT services to fail...

The "As a Service" Business Model

The majority of IoT services are being deployed with an as-a-service (AaS) business model, or many are converting their existing services to AaS. It is a term that is often used but frequently misunderstood in the IoT space. The purpose of this chapter is to introduce the reader to the most important concepts of this business model. It is more complex than the more traditional capex business models and is not a good fit for all IoT business scenarios. Each IoT service must be analyzed to assess its suitability to understand whether it is the best option to achieve the end goal, which is a successful business. (See Chapter 4 for additional information.) Many IoT services should consider the option of starting with a capex model and evolving to AaS as they gain a better understanding of their specific business scenario.

The first concept to understand with an AaS model is that the customer is buying a capability rather than a product. The customer should not be concerned with the internal details of how this capability is delivered. The service provider is delivering value to the customer by managing

© Barry Haughian 2018
B. Haughian, *Design, Launch, and Scale IoT Services*,
https://doi.org/10.1007/978-1-4842-3712-0_9

this complexity, thus allowing the customer to concentrate on their core business. For example, energy providers have a core business of producing and delivering energy to homes. A key supporting process is the ability to read the meter data and produce bills, but it is not their core expertise. Implementing the infrastructure, technology, processes, and personnel required to create and deliver bills is now being outsourced to IoT service providers. The energy providers require this capability but don't want to manage the complexity of how it is achieved.

The second concept to understand is that if a vendor sells a product, it has a value to their customer, and this value increases with usage. This increased value is usually not passed back to the vendor in a capex model, but it is in an AaS model. In the previous example, as the energy provider delivers energy to more homes, they will require an increase in the number of meter readings to create the bills. The capability they require from the meter-reading service increases, and the provider of the service should be rewarded. The service provider will not have significant increases in costs as the volumes increase, but they will be rewarded by offering increased capability to the energy provider. The AaS business model fits well with most IoT services as they are designed for scale, and this scaling is directly reflected in the revenue back to the service provider. The service provider has a recurring revenue based on the delivery of the meter-reading rather than one off product sale.

Finally, one should consider that the AaS business model requires a long-term business view. This model implies the service provider is investing in the success of the customer's business. In many cases, it is a partnership rather than a traditional vendor/customer model. As the customer's deployment of the service increases (via device deployment), the customer's revenue will increase. This in turn is reflected in increased sales for the service provider. If the initial cost for the service is too high, it can hinder growth, therefore, service provider needs to consider this in the commercial model.

Understanding AaS vs. Capex

The AaS business model is often described as a "pay-as-you-grow" model. This allows the customer to avail of the service without a large up-front expenditure. The implication of this is key to IoT because it allows startup companies or small and medium-sized businesses to avail of IoT services. The customer base is increased compared to a capex model because they can have a low entry cost and pay only for usage. Another key advantage is that AaS enables the service provider to manage their business with a predictable recurring revenue. The peaks and troughs associated with the capex model are usually less profound in an AaS model due to recurring revenue. This reduces complexity for managing the financial and growth targets of the business.

An AaS model is often described as moving from a capex to opex model, which is not strictly true. The cost of producing the service is taken up front, which is capex, but further opex costs are incurred to operate the service after it has been launched. The revenue generated from each customer is spread out over the period of the contract and should increase as more devices and services are deployed. The service provider receives less revenue in the early stages of a service deployment, but the AaS model generally will prove to be more profitable than capex. Another implication for cash flow that must be considered is that the customer pays only for the service usage in an AaS model. In a capex model, they are often paying for capacity not being used.

One should not rule out capex models for IoT services; established companies that prefer to purchase an IoT service as a product and have the capital to do so may not want to enter into an AaS model. Often, they will have existing support organizations that are working with IoT products in a capex model and want to continue with this approach. Selling the IoT service in a capex model can generate revenue before the service has scaled and can ease cash flow issues for service providers.

Figures 9-1 and 9-2 illustrate an AaS business model's financial graph. It can be quite beneficial for IoT services to create similar charts because it can simplify the process of business modeling. The following are the key points to be illustrated from this example:

- The business reaches a profit after three to four quarters when sales surpass the sum of opex and capex.

- The capex has a moderate increase because of the rollout of devices and the evolution of the service with new features.

- The opex is key; it remains relatively flat in an AaS business model. If it increases matching the device rollout, the business may never become profitable.

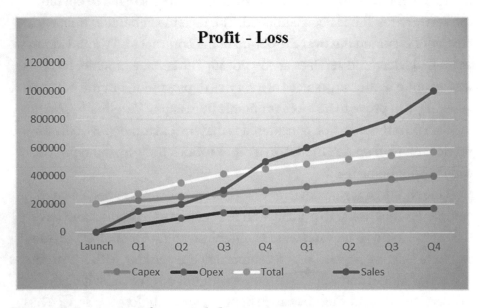

Figure 9-1. *An AaS financial chart*

Cost	Launch	Q1	Q2	Q3	Q4	Q1	Q2	Q3	Q4
Capex	200000	225000	250000	275000	300000	325000	350000	375000	400000
Opex	0	50000	100000	140000	150000	160000	170000	170000	170000
Total	200000	275000	350000	415000	450000	485000	520000	545000	570000
Sales	0	150000	200000	300000	500000	600000	700000	800000	1000000

Figure 9-2. *The AaS financial chart details*

Initial Costs: The first calculations required by service providers are the development and operating costs of the service. The development and lifecycle management service costs should be spread across all customers. If the service provider estimates ten customers in the first year of deployment, then the service development costs to be allocated for each customer for year 1 could be divided by a factor of up to 10. This results in the service being more attractive for customers at service launch; in other words, all the costs are not being charged to the first customers. It increases risk for the service provider as they are charging based on the customer forecast. The implication is that service provider won't recover their initial investment until the forecasted customer volumes have been reached.

Deployment Costs: The cost of deploying the service can be either incorporated into the price per device or charged directly to the customer based on time and material. This is where the service provider should consider whether making a profit on the deployment costs is the correct strategy. IoT services are most successful with scale, and if deployment costs are prohibitive for customers, it may hinder the scaling of the service.

Operational Costs: The final calculations are the operational costs required to deliver the service according to the SLA. If the service is designed and well managed, these costs will be divided across each customer and remain relatively flat as the service grows.

The price of the service can be "value based" where the service owner calculates the value to the customer and sells according to this. This should maximize profits, but the challenge is that it can be difficult to calculate. Often, I recommend cost-based pricing to be used in the early stages of deployment where the service provider calculates the costs and adds their margin. This should ensure the business is successful in its infancy, and as the service provider gains experience understanding the value to different customers, they can switch to a value-based pricing model as the service scales.

Keys for Success in an IoT Business

The following are keys for success:

- **Scaling**: The IoT is a numbers game, and services must be designed to facilitate scaling. Scaling should be considered from a technical and operational perspective with forecasts based on both customer and device volumes.

- **Operations**: Operational costs must remain relatively flat as the service grows in terms of customers and devices. Costs can increase as new features are implemented, but they should not increase significantly unless it is in-line with the business model.

- **Security**: The cost for security must be factored in to the business case. This is important to ensure security levels match the needs of the service. If too much is spent on security, it can destroy the business case.

- **Ecosystem**: Planning for an ecosystem and investing the time and effort to develop it with partners may not be a priority at launch, but it will ultimately lead to improved growth and service exposure.

- **Speed**: The speed and ease with which new customers and devices can be added to the service will ultimately determine the scalability.

- **Automation**: Most IoT services will not be able to control costs as the volumes grow without consistently implementing new automated processes. This needs to be considered from all service aspects including the addition of new customers, devices, and features. Automation will reduce operational effort, complexity and cost.

- **Architecture**: A layered modular architecture with clear interfaces between modules is fundamental for the lifecycle management of IoT services. It will be key for managing complexity as the services expand and evolve.

Key Challenges for a Successful IoT Business

The following are the key challenges:

- **Service description**: An unclear service description will impact customer satisfaction. Discussions will center on what is available as part of the service rather than on how to use and grow the service.

- **Technical focus**: If the discussions with the customer focus on the technical solution and components within an IoT service, it can distract from the business. The discussions must be centered on what the service provides, not how it is implemented.

- **Quality of service**: Managing the growth in terms of geographical location must be considered. If a distributed system is not designed, it may not be possible to ensure quality of service is equal irrespective of location. This will hinder growth.

- **IPR**: Not protecting the IoT service assets and monetizing on them ultimately allows competitors, partners, and possibly customers to take advantage of the service without being charged, reducing the chances of success.

- **Customizations**: If too many customizations are introduced, it impacts the opportunities for scaling and has a negative impact on operations in terms of complexity and cost.

- **Regulation**: Not understanding local regulations before launching a service in a new market can impact the service deployment, requiring specific local deployments that are customised.

- **Complexity**: The complexity of the service implementation should be hidden from the customer, and therefore the service should be intuitive and easy to operate from the end-user perspective.

CHAPTER 10

The Current and Future Status of the IoT

The following sections are a series of interviews with industry experts who give their views on the IoT revolution. I use some of these insights to try to draw some conclusions about the future of IoT. One thing seems to be certain: there doesn't exist one view on the future of the IoT. We have a long journey to follow the evolution path of IoT. For further reading, see Ref. 20, "10 Questions to Ask an IoT Platform Provider."[1]

Nokia: Grant Marshall, VP of Supply Network and Engineering

Where are we with IoT? Is it fulfilling your expectations?

Nokia has been working toward Industry 4.0 for some time. We have driven a theme in our supply chain that focuses on the following key areas: digitalization, analytics, robotics, and transparency. As we deploy more

---

[1] 10 Questions to Ask an IoT Platform Provider www.engineering.com.

© Barry Haughian 2018
B. Haughian, *Design, Launch, and Scale IoT Services*,
https://doi.org/10.1007/978-1-4842-3712-0_10

IoT devices, more automation cells, and more process automation, data has been key to understand where to focus, make changes, and observe the impact. The IoT was the vehicle to achieve significant improvement in our productivity.

How will it impact Industry 4.0?

Industry 4.0 needs significant IoT solutions to deliver on its expectations of the IoT for digitalization, IoT for automation, and IoT for support and visualization. The biggest challenge will be the interoperation of the IoT with existing legacy systems and interoperation between the IoT. Thousands of IoT devices from 40 to 50 different companies may work together in one ecosystem.

How will AR and AI evolve with the IoT?

Augmented reality is the next big game changer. AR will be used in a multiple of applications.

- AR factory work instructions (a guaranteed understanding of work steps)

- AR picklists (guaranteed correct picking for work orders)

- AR guided to picking locations (guaranteed fast find of material for picking)

- AR repair instruction (aided repair instruction and feedback on next steps)

- External site AR troubleshooting

Artificial intelligence is closely tied to data. AI requires data to make and draw conclusions that provide recommendations. IoT sensors, AR video feeds, and video analytics, coupled with machine learning and the M2M communications of today, give AI the data needed to understand business flows and determine correlation and causation to recommend action for improvement. As humans can't process the amount of data that AI systems are now consuming, we will see a lot of innovation from AI.

What are the biggest challenges?

One of the challenges today is connectivity. Existing connectivity relies on legacy architectures such as cables, Wi-Fi, Bluetooth, ZigBee, etc., all of which work but have limitations. The simple example is with cables. When scaling IoT from 50 to 60 IoT devices today connected with cables to thousands of devices tomorrow, cables simply do not scale. We have tried private LTE networking as a precursor to 5G, and this works perfectly except has the existing challenge of getting access to the spectrum. By using 5G, guard bands, and so on, these challenges disappear, and private networking becomes a reality. However, in my view, obtaining efficient interoperability between hundreds of different IoT companies to a single management system and between IoT devices is a challenge that is aggressively being worked on today. Open ecosystems and cooperation with competition will be the key to success. The final challenge is the misuse of the IoT. If companies deploy thousands of IoT devices without a strategy on what data they need or want and what an AI solution will provide them, they may over-engineer the solutions and add unwanted costs. In addition, IoT companies will not understand what to do with data and how to realize actual benefit/improvements.

What are the implications of 5G for the IoT?

5G should enable massive growth for the IoT. Many of the bottlenecks for large-scale deployment will disappear. I believe we are at a perfect alignment of opportunity and timing. The IoT can scale now with existing infrastructure. This will allow companies to learn, try, and adapt their business processes to the IoT. When private 5G networks can be deployed, a lot of the IoT challenges with interoperability issues will be resolved. IoT devices can be embedded with 5G wireless technology. This will make mass deployment as simple as device registration, with increased security, low latency, and increased edge computing.

What is the role of ecosystems in the IoT?

Ecosystems are the key to success. Industry 4.0 is not about a single-solution environment. It is about a multivendor environment. If companies do not embrace an open ecosystem, they simply will not be able to innovate at the pace expected.

The IoT and 5G are key pillars to the fourth industrial revolution. They will change the concepts of legacy telecommunication going forward. The IoT itself has already made significant headway, well ahead of 5G.

Microsoft: Luis (Tayo) Carvalhal, Global Black Belt IoT

Where are we with the IoT? Is it fulfilling your expectations?

The IoT is expected to provide some important foundations for digital transformation, and it will have a profound effect on our world. As such, it is inevitable that some aspects of society will act with more agility than others. For example, discrete manufacturing has always been at the forefront of automation, and this is where most innovation has been observed in line with my expectations.

What are the technology challenges for IoT growth?

IoT is not a technology-driven revolution; it is a social one. As such, the biggest challenges are the inertia from some parts of society that will be slow in adapting to the change. It is quite safe to say that today technology is one step ahead, and society needs to play catch-up. However, this is not a view shared everywhere, and many IoT innovations are still perceived as complex, mostly with regard to security, integration with legacy system, costs, and ability to scale.

How are cloud services supporting the IoT revolution?

Without pervasive cloud computing, the IoT will never materialize. Cloud services provide mechanisms that allow IoT experiments (proofs of concept, pilots) to be executed cheap and fast, while giving the assurance that once an experiment is successfully executed, it will naturally scale to the level required by the application.

What are the implications of AI and AR advances for IoT services?

The IoT will bring automation to a completely new level. Its chattiness provides a flow of information that can't be matched by humans in terms of responsiveness and decision-making. As an example, one of the most important applications in these early stages of IoT implementation is predictive maintenance in the industry vertical. AR plays a less driving factor at this stage, mostly because it is still feels awkward for humans to immerse in its applications. However, as we naturally become more accustomed to AR, it will become an important part of IoT applications.

How will 5G impact IoT services?

The IoT expects ubiquitous and fewer resources consuming connectivity. 5G has made some promises in these respects. Having said that, it has taken a long time to materialize, and society has not waited for it. To the contrary, in respect to earlier 3GPP releases, this time it will face other technologies that are real contenders. However, the mobile telecom ecosystem is strong and will fill a needed role in the complete IoT value chain.

What do you expect for the future of connected devices?

It is clear that any device that can provide value to any aspect of society by being connected will be connected. In its initial phase, it will be in the scale of tens of billions, but as it gets democratized and spreads to all strata of society, it will reach much higher numbers. The question is not how many, but *when* will everything be connected?

Ericsson: Miguel Blockstrand, Head of IoT DCP

What are the key benefits of connectivity management?

The revenues generated per M2M or IoT device require the implementation of a new business model to reduce capex and opex. Connectivity management platforms reduce opex by automating and offshoring connectivity management to customers. Economies of scale can be achieved by using the multitenant platforms that share resources as the business scales.

What are the key challenges for IoT services?

Scale will not happen without a clear strategy, and this requires vertical industry knowledge; therefore, IoT service providers need to incorporate this knowledge into their service design, GTM strategies, and growth plans. Targeting specific verticals where the knowledge exists or through partnerships will be key for successful IoT services.

Incorporating near edge computing and distributed systems will be key for new services to enable scaling. Regulations are changing, which will restrict the flexibility to store certain types of IoT data. Near edge computing can overcome many of the obstacles as well as provide instant response capabilities for IoT services.

What is the future of the IoT?

Industry 4.0 is upon us; it may incorporate the IoT into a bigger concept, and it will rely on IoT services to drive it to its full potential. As IoT services scale, they will have to become more efficient. Current ways of working will not be sufficient in the future, and this is where concepts like Industry 4.0 need to take hold. Managing or producing hundreds of thousands or millions of devices presents unique challenges, and the technology is there to support this. IoT service owners will have to constantly incorporate new technology. The IoT services will have to be flexible enough to constantly adapt to the rapidly changing landscape.

What is one key learning from your IoT journey?

The consumer end applications are the key GTM tool for platform providers for promoting platforms and services. The technology behind the service is irrelevant for most users. Most of the population has become tech savvy. We have become knowledgeable in managing applications and the associated technology because of the careful design of the end-user interfaces. This will continue to present challenges and opportunities for IoT services as the pace of change and volume of new services increase.

The Future

There are as many predictions on the future of IoT as there are services, and very little consensus. Many services are being classed as IoT to take advantage of the hype, but we will see this hype die down, and ultimately, I expect many of these services will not be sustainable. We will continue to see phenomenal growth in the numbers of new services, which will be matched by an increase in supporting services, in other words, the building blocks of the IoT. There will be significant development with devices, communication technologies, cloud services, and so on. Therefore, the opportunities for innovative services should continue to increase, and many will become fundamental in our daily lives.

I expect the following are the most likely trends for the IoT in the coming years:

- More connectivity options will be available for IoT services with the rollout of NB-IoT/LTE-M from traditional telecommunication providers competing with Lora, Sigfox, and so on. Longer-term connectivity capacity will be key as we scale on devices. 5G shows a lot of promise, but the initial costs may be prohibitive for many IoT services.

- We are already seeing significant hype in artificial intelligence (AI) and augmented reality (AR) services, and this can be expected to continue. The development costs and complexity will decrease, but there will still be a significant challenge of how to monetize successfully (For further reading, see Ref. 21, "80 percent of organisations set to invest in AI."[2]).

- We will see an increase in edge technology as costs for devices decrease, and many cloud services will offer options for deployment on edge devices. This presents challenges and opportunities for IoT services managing the business cost/benefit of introducing edge technology.

- New regulations are being introduced as governments try to catch up with the Internet and IoT revolutions. IoT services will have to gain a better understanding of the implications of new laws. For example, there doesn't seem to be a broad or clear understanding of the implications of the EU's GDPR.

- There are many predictions for blockchain to be introduced in IoT services as a security feature. There is still a lot of hype surrounding this technology, and it remains to be seen if IoT service owners will be able to manage the cost/benefit. As mentioned previously, the cost of not having a secure service can be much higher than the required investment if data is compromised.

- There are many predictions for the increase in use of big data, but I suspect that most IoT services will not have sufficient data for it to be "big". It is more likely that IoT will thrive with smaller, less complex but more innovative use cases. Intelligent use of data will be fundamental for success, but that doesn't require large volumes.

---

[2]80 percent of organisations set to invest in AI https://internetofbusiness.com.

- Industry 4.0 will cause a mini-revolution that will impact directly the complexity, cost, and effort required to manufacture and deploy IoT devices. It will offer a decrease in the costs required to create and deploy the services, ultimately expanding the range of use cases and applicable industries.

- Security will always be a challenge for IoT services, and with each security breach making the news the requirements on IoT services will increase. Managing the investments in IoT security will be an ever-increasing challenge for IoT services.

- The number of IoT platforms available is staggering, and we may see a consolidation in the future. The costs will continue to decrease, and many may become industry vertical specific except for a few big players.

- Operational management will become an issue as device volumes increase. The ability to control operational costs and activities will remain key for success. The careful selection of supporting tools (such as inventory management software) will become more complex as the number of options increase.

- We should expect to see an increase in IoT ecosystems, with many services combining technology from partners to create services. Understanding the real value of being part of an ecosystem will be increasingly important and complex but key for success.

APPENDIX A

Service Description

Intelligent Transport Services

This appendix provides a service description of the an Intelligent Transport Service (ITS) for illustration purposes only. This document is an example of a contractual document.

Figure A-1. *ITS*

Introduction

Intelligent Transport Service offers a suite of mobile web-based services to transport companies, (referred to as "Operators" in this document), that enable the efficient management of their transport business. These services

© Barry Haughian 2018
B. Haughian, *Design, Launch, and Scale IoT Services*,
https://doi.org/10.1007/978-1-4842-3712-0

can be used by the Operators to reduce costs, increase customer satisfaction, and contribute to the overall success of the business.

These services can also be used by the transport regulatory authorities to have instant access to precise information related to Operator incomes, passenger volumes, profiles, vehicle telematics information.

Note   This contract does not specify the type of Operator as the service could be used in multiple transport scenarios. The service description is a contractual document; the benefits of the service do not need to be explained in detail here.

ITS services are delivered via the deployment of ITS hardware and software that can be accessed via mobile devices. These include onboard vehicle devices for drivers, payment devices for passengers, ITS Internet portals for passengers, and ITS management portals used by Operator management.

The Intelligent Transport Service suite consists of the following services (see Figure A-2):

- **ITS enterprise services offer the following services to the Operator and passengers**:

    i.   The Enterprise Fleet Management service enables the Operator to track vehicle positions, monitor active vehicles, manage planned traffic routes, track journey times, and produce punctuality reports. It offers intelligent planning of routes and management of resources to maximize efficiency and reduce operational costs.

    ii. The Automated Fare Collection service offers the ability for passengers to use their smartphones for ticket reservations and payment of journeys. The Operator can track payments and automatically generate financial records for business management.

iii. The Real-Time Passenger Information service offers passengers the ability to receive real-time information regarding the bus locations, journey times, and real-time traffic information.

- **ITS management services**: These services provide operational and service management capabilities for Operators.

- **ITS initial setup services**: These services provide project-based activities that install ITS hardware and software required to enable the Operator and their customers to avail of the ITS services. Additional advanced setup services integrating with legacy systems are also available upon request.

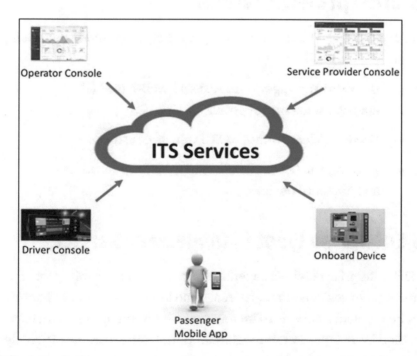

Figure A-2. ITS components

- **Driver console**: This includes hardware and software enabling bidirectional communication with drivers.

- **Mobile app**: This software enables passengers to purchase tickets and access real-time fleet information.

- **Onboard device**: This is hardware enabling ticket validation.

- **Operator console**: This is software offering operational and business tools.

- **Service provider console**: This is software offering operational management functions.

ITS Enterprise Services

The ITS services can be accessed using a variety of methods depending on the user.

- **Operator management**: Access a web-based ITS management control portal.

- **Drivers**: Access onboard ITS vehicle consoles.

- **Passengers**: Access web-based mobile applications and payment devices.

ITS Enterprise Fleet Management Service

The ITS Enterprise Fleet Management service offers the ability for Operator management to receive real-time information on the fleet status and take corrective actions to increase efficiency and performance. It is enabled by an Operator management portal and an onboard vehicle console. The onboard vehicle console offers bidirectional communication between the vehicle and operations management portal. The console reports real-time vehicle data and can receive instructions that can be relayed to the driver. This management portal provides a dashboard with the following functionality:

- Vehicle position

- Deviation from planned routes

- Monitoring the status of bus doors

- Links to onboard installed cameras

- Access to the drivers' console displays

Note   Specific details of the devices are not included in the contract at this stage. These are presented and discussed during sales meetings in a non-contractual manner as it is expected they will evolve over time.

Automated Fare Collection Service

This is provided through onboard vehicle payment devices permitting automatic payment through secure web-based applications. It includes business support functionality to ensure efficient revenue control.

Device Payments

Onboard payment devices are fully integrated with ITS management control functions, enabling the real-time monitoring of payments. Clients can use mobile applications to refill prepaid cards and pay for journeys by swiping their phone in front of the onboard devices.

Billing Support

- Real-time billing information is available through the ITS management control portal.

- Consolidated weekly billing reports are available through the reporting functions.

- Projected revenues and fraud analysis reports are provided via big data analytics.

Note   Real-time billing must be defined in the service level agreement (SLA).

Real-Time Passenger Information

This is accessed by the Operator via the management portal and is enabled via the onboard connectivity service. Each onboard vehicle device has mobile communication functionality enabling it to send real-time passenger information to the management control function. The data is analyzed and presented to the Operator with recommendations for optimization. Passenger and revenue data is available per route on a daily, weekly, monthly, and yearly basis.

The following functionality is included in the standard service:

- Passenger volumes per vehicle

- Revenue generated per vehicle

- Real-time capacity data analysis

Passengers can access vehicle locations and the estimated time of arrival via apps and web-based applications.

ITS Management Services

ITS management services are categorized into service management and business support functions. They are accessed via web-based portals and are used by the service provider to support SLA compliance. Service management offers the tools to manage and maintain the assets required to deliver the end-to-end service. The business support functions provide the Operator with the tools required to manage the business aspects of their transportation service.

Service Management Function

This service manages the lifecycle of the software and devices including resource management. It is offered using local and global resources providing the following capabilities:

- Deploy, integrate, and maintain vehicle onboard devices

- Deploy, integrate, and maintain vehicle onboard point-of-sale devices

- Operator support service desk for Automatic Fare Collection service

- Distribution of Automatic Fare Collection cards

- Physical integration of SIM cards

- First-line support for fault management

Note An explanation of the functionality for each type of device may be required, but the description should be limited in contractually binding documents. Too much detail reduces the flexibility of the service provider to change devices in future releases.

Business Support Services

These services are provided via web-based tools that are accessed via the business support portal:

- Data and device management

- Lightweight customer relation management

- Deployment, hosting, and lifecycle management

- Real-time/predictive data analytics

- Billing and subscription management

- Multimediation and settlements management

- Asset management

- Logging and monitoring

- Training and knowledge transfer

- All connectivity requirements, including local and international

Initial Setup Services

These services include the fulfilment activities that are performed by the service provider deployment teams to configure the ITS service for the Operator and their end customers.

Note   The Initial setup services must be contractual as successful completion of these services should trigger commercial acceptance, operation of the service and payments toward the service provider.

The following prerequisites must be completed before the setup services can begin execution:

- The Operator has provided a complete and unambiguous set of configuration data as specified in the data collection documents.

- The Operator has provided connectivity to the ITS service gateway.

- The Operator has accepted the provided time slot for delivering the service.

- The Operator has appointed an interface to act as single point of coordination toward the delivery team and stakeholders.

The Initial setup services are executed with the following scope:

- Implement onboarding of devices in five vehicles.

- Implement the service portal for the Operator.

- Perform acceptance tests of the onboarded devices.

- Training is provided as follows:

  - On one occasion

  - On-site, at Operator premises

  - Maximum class size of 15 participants

Note   The Operator can request an increase in scope with additional services and cost, but these should be agreed on before execution of this service.

Service Access

The following sections outline the conditions under which the service may be accessed.

Service Demarcation Points

The service demarcation point for Intelligent Transport Service is the service gateway through which the service is delivered. This is the point from where the SLA is measured.

Note   The service provider cannot control the quality of the mobile communication and access environment into the service demarcation point. Therefore, the SLA must include a clause to state KPI measurements for the services being delivered exclude mobile communication measurements.

Service Security Management

The Operator is responsible for securing the operational capabilities and operational systems integrity as defined in the security policy.

The Operator is responsible for securing the integrity of the following data attributes:

- Subscription data linked to the IMSI and MSISDN SIM identities

- Transaction (payload) data

- Charging and billing records

- Tariff plans

- CRM data

Security Policy

The Operator is responsible for the security policy within the following domains:

- Intelligent Transport System production sites and premises security

- Management tools and IT security

- Operational staff and access rights–related security

Hours of Operation

The service will operate 24 hours a day, 7 days a week, and 365 days a year.

The service provider will deliver the ITS services according to the service level agreement.

Definitions, Acronyms, and Abbreviations

- **BSS**: Business support system

- **Operator**: Customer contracting the ITS service

- **CRM**: Customer relation management

- **HW**: Hardware

- **ITS service gate**: The gateway for receiving all mobile communication

- **IMSI**: International Mobile Subscriber Identity; uniquely identifies a mobile device

- **ITS**: Intelligent Transport Service

- **KPI**: Key performance indicator

- **MSISDN**: Mobile Station International Subscriber Directory Number

- **SLA**: Service level agreement

- **SPOC**: Single point of contact

- **SW**: Software

APPENDIX B

Service Level Agreement

Figure B-1. *ITS*

Service Performance

The service provider is responsible for delivering the service described in the service description. The performance of the service will be measured by the indicators defined in this document.

© Barry Haughian 2018
B. Haughian, *Design, Launch, and Scale IoT Services*,
https://doi.org/10.1007/978-1-4842-3712-0

Key Performance Indicators

The KPIs will be used to measure the quality of the Intelligent Transport Service, further referred to as ITS KPIs in this document.

The service provider will hold monthly performance review meetings with the customer.

The customer/transport operator will be (referred to as the "Operator" in this document) required to review the performance of the KPIs with the service provider.

Main KPI Specification

Table B-1. *KPI Specification*

KPI	Service Level Measurement	Expected Service Level Target	Service Credits
ITS onboard service availability	Aggregation of the ITS service availability KPIs	Comply	No
ITS service management availability	Aggregation of the ITS business support availability KPIs	Comply	No
ITS billing	Aggregation of the ITS billing KPIs	Comply	Yes

Note Service credits are given to Operators that can be used to reduce monthly service fees. In this service, billing services are defined as the only KPI that will result in service credits.

Service Availability

Service availability is measured by the monitoring tools of the service provider. ITS availability will be measured by each calendar month, calculated as defined in Table B-2.

Planned outages and other KPI exclusions should be defined clearly and exempt from such measurements.

Note   There can be a tendency to overcomplicate measurements. A smaller number of KPIs giving an accurate measurement of service performance is crucial for managing Operator expectations.

Table B-2.   *Service Availability*

KPI	Value
Planned service availability	= Available time in month – Actual downtime within a service window
Actual service availability	= Planned service availability – Unscheduled downtime
Service availability level (%)	= Actual service availability / Planned service availability

Aggregation Method

The main KPIs are aggregated in the following way:

- If all the KPIs belonging to an aggregation group are above target, the aggregated target is Comply.

- If any of the service KPIs are below target, the aggregated target is Not Comply.

- In such cases, the KPIs below target will be presented with the actual value of the KPI not meeting the agreed target.

Service Capacity Expansion

The Operator will provide a written forecast prior to requesting any expansion of an ITS service. The service provider will analyze the forecast and the resulting expansion requirements. The parties will discuss the outcome of the analysis and, if mutually agreed by the all parties, will initiate the capacity expansion process.

For indicative purposes:

- The expansions requiring virtual resources in the ITS system sites may take four to six weeks.

- The expansions requiring physical hardware may take six to twelve weeks and are dependent on hardware lead-time availability when ordering.

ITS Maintenance Windows

The service provider reserves the right to carry out scheduled maintenance activities in line with the ITS operational activities and road map planning. It is intended that one maintenance window will be planned for each calendar month. Maintenance windows will have a maximum downtime of one hour.

Planned Downtime

Due to the nature and scope of the maintenance activities, it may be necessary for planned downtime to occur within the maintenance window. In cases where planned downtime is necessary and there is an expected interruption of services, the service provider will notify the Operator no less than ten days prior to the planned activities. All activities should take place in non-peak traffic hours except in the case of an emergency update being required where planned downtime is necessary as part of the implementation procedure. In this case, the Operator will be notified at the first available opportunity before the emergency update is applied. See Table B-3.

Table B-3. *Planned Downtime*

Description	Definition	Comment
Maintenance window	A predefined time where maintenance is performed.	12 per calendar year.
Maintenance window duration	Each planned maintenance window will have a maximum duration of six hours to ensure all maintenance activities can be completed.	72 hours per calendar year.
Planned downtime	The length of time the service is impacted within the maintenance window.	1 hour per maintenance window
ITS availability	Infrastructure within the ITS providing the service.	Planned downtime for the calendar year must not exceed more than 12 hours in total.

Reporting and Service Availability KPIs

The following sections specify the report and service availability KPIs.

Reporting

Reports will be made available to the Operator no later than seven business days after the end of each calendar month. The service provider will distribute a report describing the service performance compliance with the KPIs. This report will be reviewed during the monthly performance review meetings.

KPI compliance or non-compliance is defined using the lowest single calculated KPI to represent the overall main KPI availability.

Excluded from KPI Measurements

The following disturbances will fall outside the scope of KPI measurements. This includes but is not limited to the following:

- Planned downtime for maintenance or installation
- Force majeure
- Equipment or services outside the demarcation point
- Any matter set out in warranty commitments

ITS Onboard Service Availability KPIs

Table B-4. *Onboard Service Availability*

Service Level	KPI	Description	Formula	Target	Major/Minor
ITS management service	Service availability	The ITS platform is considered unavailable for one minute if all continuous attempts to send or receive messages or perform device identity operations throughout the minute either return an error code or do not result in a success code within ten minutes.	Availability % = ((Total minutes – Unavailable minutes) / Total minutes) * 100)	>= 99%	Major
Automatic fare collection	Service availability	KPI measures the accessibility of data related to automatic fare collection with respect to post-processing and financial report reconciliation.	Success rate % = Completed reports availability	>= 99% success rate	Major
Real-time passenger information	Available through portal and apps	The KPI measures the ability of a user to access a report.	Success rate % = Reports availability	<= 0.5 % cutoff failure rate >= 99.5% success rate	Major

ITS Service Management KPIs

Table B-5. *Service Management KPIs*

Service Level	KPI	Description	Formula	Target	Major/ Minor
Service management portal	Service portal availability	KPI measures the availably of the service portal. An HTTP GET is issued every 60 seconds from the HTTP client toward the portal's launch page. If the portal is not reachable within 30 seconds of being contacted, it is considered unavailable.	Availability % = ((Total minutes – Unavailable minutes) / Total minutes) * 100)	>= 99 %	Major
Business support service portal	Service portal availability	KPI measures the availably of the service portal. An HTTP GET is issued every 60 seconds from the HTTP client toward the portal's launch page. If the portal is not reachable within 30 seconds of being contacted, it is considered unavailable.	Availability % = ((Total minutes – Unavailable minutes) / Total minutes) * 100)	>= 99 %	Major

(continued)

Table B-5. (*continued*)

Service Level	KPI	Description	Formula	Target	Major/ Minor
API	API availability	KPI measures the availability of the API to execute service requests. The API availability KPI measures the accessibility of the API from the Internet. A query subscriber request is issued every 60 seconds from the API client toward the ITS API interface. If no response is received within 30 seconds of the request being sent, the API is considered unavailable. If an invalid or malformed response is received, the API is also considered unavailable, effectively providing verification toward the relevant internal systems.	Availability % = ((Total minutes − Unavailable minutes) / Total minutes) * 100)	>= 99 %	Major
Service request	Service request execution lead time	Measured during the calendar month of the time between submission and completion by the ITS for each service request. A service request is defined as a request received for the Operator to change the existing service. Communication outside the ITS demarcation point is not part of the measurement.	Time of completion = Completion time − Submission time		Minor

Note   Thirty seconds is selected to determine whether the portal can be accessed during the reporting time interval. The round-trip time is measured and reported in the service portal and API.

ITS Billing KPIs

Table B-6.   *Billing KPIs*

Service Level	KPI	Description	Formula	Target	Major/ Minor
Billing	Customer ability to purchase tickets	KPI measures the availability of tickets purchases.	Availability of ticket purchasing app	100%	Major
Billing reports	Billing reports available within 72 hours of month end	KPI measures the availability of all Operator-related billing information to be transferred to the nominated storage system of the operator within 72 hours of the completion of the monthly billing cycle (excluding backlog reports and suspense reports, if applicable).	100% of all Operator-related billing information available in the Operator storage system	100%	Major

Other Performance Indicators

The following sections highlight miscellaneous performance indicators.

Incident Categorization

Table B-7. *Severity Levels of an Incident*

Severity Level	Short Description of Overall Services Impact	Business Impact Summary
1 – Critical	Loss or severe degradation of service. The incident may impact Operator image because it will lead to service value deterioration.	Legal restriction not fulfilled. Service security or data/ confidentiality is breached. An incident affecting critical systems/applications, or feature/ function that is impacting all end customers. Service impacts that result in revenue loss. The ITS service is not available.
2 – High	Degradation of service; failure on a frequent or intermittent basis; workaround unsatisfactory in near-term. Loss of resilience/redundancy. The incident prevents a major number of customers from fully using the intended functions of the service.	An incident affecting critical systems/applications, or feature/ function that is the subject of a marketing promotion impacting major number of consumers. Slow response from the ITS service.

(*continued*)

Table B-7. (*continued*)

Severity Level	Short Description of Overall Services Impact	Business Impact Summary
3 – Low	Minor hosted service-related incidents. The incident prevents a minor number of customers from fully using the intended functions of the service.	Usage issues that affect minor number of consumers. Incidents related to web-based report tool.
4 – Service Request	No impact	Operator services requests and feedback on service's look, feel, and content.

Support Availability

Support is available in accordance with the following criteria:

- 24/7 help desk (critical incidents) service monitoring

- 8 a.m. to 5 p.m. Central European Time (CET) on workdays for other support levels

Workaround Time

Table B-8. *Workaround Time*

Severity Level	Remedy Time
1 – Critical (Emergency)	4 hours
2 – High	24 hours
3 – Low	7 business days

Permanent Solution

Table B-9. *Permanent Solution*

Severity Level	Solution Time
1 – Critical (Emergency)	Solution implemented within 10 business days
2 – High	Solution implemented within 20 business days
3 – Low	Solution implemented within 80 business days
4 – Service Request	When ready or agreed on wIth customer

Service Request Fulfillment

Table B-10. *Service Request Fulfillment*

Fulfilment Request Level	Fulfilment Request Description	SLA
Validation	Validation of the service request	Within one to three business days after submitting the full details of the service request in the service portal
Basic establishment	Set up and provision with low complexity	Within five business days after validation of input
Advanced establishment	Setup and provision with very advanced complexity	Within ten business days after validation of input
Complex establishment	Setup and provision with very high complexity	Within 15 business days after validation of input

Reporting and Statistics

Table B-11. *Reporting and Statistics*

Report	Delivery Interval
Preliminary Incident Report for Severity 1 (Emergency)	One to two business days
Final Incident Report for Severity 1 (Emergency)	30 business days
Service Performance and Availability Report	Monthly
Service Request Report	Monthly

APPENDIX C

Operational Framework

Figure C-1. *ITS*

General

This document provides an operational framework for the Intelligent Transport Service. The Head of Operations is responsible for the maintenance of this document to ensure it reflects the current operational structure of ITS.

© Barry Haughian 2018
B. Haughian, *Design, Launch, and Scale IoT Services*,
https://doi.org/10.1007/978-1-4842-3712-0

This is document is for internal use only.

The operational framework outlines the organizations, interfaces, and functions required to launch and operate the Intelligent Transport Service.

The operational functions are delivered by the service delivery and operations (SD&O) organization that coordinates the delivery activities from supporting organizations. The core organization is defined as follows:

- Head of Operations

- Operations management team

- DevOps

- Engineering function

- Service desk

Note   Many SD&O models include a service desk as a core function. For the ITS model, it is considered core even though it is delivered by another organization.

These SD&O organizations combine with external organizations to implement the functions required to deliver and operate the Intelligent Transport Service.

- Operations management

- Service assurance

- Demand management

Figure C-2 illustrates a high-level overview of the service components that fall within the scope of this operational framework.

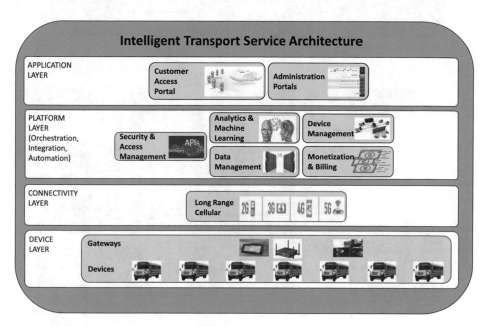

Figure C-2. *Architecture overview*

Operational Overview

The SD&O organization implements the central operational functions interfacing with stakeholders and external contributors to deliver the service. Figure C-3 illustrates the interfaces between the organizations that deliver and operate the Intelligent Transport Service as specified in the contractual documents. These interfaces are outlined in the agreements between the contributing organizations, i.e., the working level agreements (WLAs) and the service level agreements (SLAs).

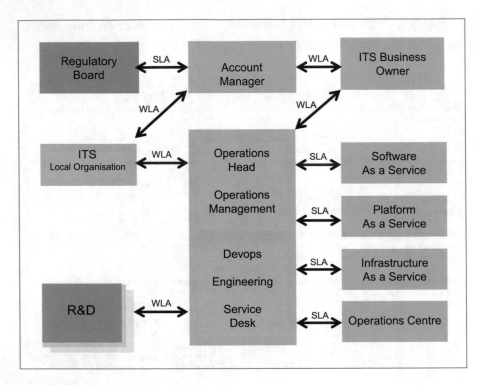

Figure C-3. *Operational interfaces*

The organizations are defined as follows

- **Regulatory board**: The public organization that defines the regulatory terms and conditions (T&C) under which the service may operate.

- **Account manager(s)**: The commercial organization responsible for the service toward specific customers.

- **ITS business owner**: Responsible for the profit and loss (P&L) of the service toward all customers. Accountable for the service definition (scope and service level agreements), commercial T&C, and service delivery and operations.

- **ITS local SD&O**: Responsible for local service delivery and operational activities (as agreed on by the central operations functions). Manages all local activities including hardware maintenance and support.

- **Operations Head**: Overall responsibility for service delivery and operations for all customers.

- **Operations Management**: Central function managing and coordinating service delivery for all customers. Responsibilities include the following:

  - Service delivery management (reporting, statistics, KPIs, etc.)

  - Contract management

  - Interface and process management

  - Service level management

  - Fraud

- **DevOps**: Responsible for supporting the technical development and maintenance of the service including all customer implementations.

  - Technical requirements support

  - Customizations and life cycle management

  - Customer service life cycle management

  - Assurance support

- **Engineering**: Responsible for customer deployments including the following:

  - Software deployment

  - Configuration management

  - Site management

  - Capacity planning/performance/optimization

- **Software as a service**: Provides software in an "as a service" model.

- **Platform as a service**: Provides platform components in an "as a service" model.

- **Infrastructure as a service**: Provides infrastructure components in an "as a service" model.

- **Operations center**: Responsible for routine service delivery and operations activities to ensure the service performs according to the SLA.

- **R&D**: Research and development scrum teams responsible for development of the service.

Agreements

The following are the agreements:

- **Service level agreements**: A contract is signed between the service owners and external organizations.

  - **Regulatory body/account**: The regulatory body defines requirements to be met to ensure the quality of service provided to the public.

- **SD&O/(SaaS, PaaS, IaaS)**: The SD&O organization agreements with external organizations.

- **SD&O/Operations Centre**: Organizations providing services contributing to SD&O.

- **Working Level agreements**: The contract signed between internal organizations, defining the service level agreed on by both parties. It defines the scope of the work to be delivered from each organization, the service components, and the delivery responsibility.

  - **Account/Local delivery/SD&O**: Agreement defining the local responsibilities, interfaces, and processes contributing to the delivery (as forecasted by the customer)

  - **Account/Business owner**: Agreement defining service scope and service levels according to processes and forecasted volumes

  - **Business owner/Head of Operations**: Agreement defining the service level performance and processes for forecasted volumes of all cusotmers

  - **SD&O/R&D**: Agreement for service level related to trouble ticket resolution and support for new service releases

Operational Flow Overview

Figure C-4 outlines the interaction between the stakeholders and the delivery organization for contracted ITS services.

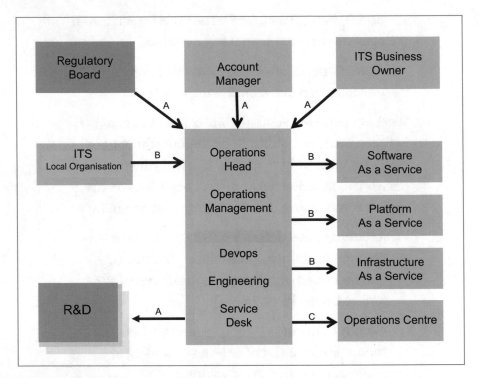

Figure C-4. *Operational interfaces*

Note   The procedures manual defines the specific contact details for each organization and should be completed before the service goes live for each customer.

- **Interface A**: Contact through e-mail or telephone as defined in procedures manual

- **Interface B**: Trouble ticket or service requests raised with CRM tool

- **Interface C**: Contact through e-mail, telephone, and CRM software

The procedures manuals will define the specific contact details for each customer and the delivery organization.

Service Delivery and Operations

SD&O is the core organization responsible for delivering and operating the Intelligent Transport Service. It contains management roles (Head of Operations and Operations Management) and delivery roles (DevOps, Engineering, and the Service desk) that own and manage activities required to deliver the service.

Head of Operations

The Operations Head has overall responsibility for delivery and operations. Duties include the following:

- Compliance with agreed budget for delivery and operations activities

- Overall responsibility for operational performance KPIs

- Responsible for defining and managing the operational organization structure including dimensioning

- Accountable for adherence of the working and service level agreements toward stakeholders and customers

Operations Management

Operations management is responsible for the performance of the functions operations assurance and demand management. The organization consists of service managers who monitor and manage the performance of the services towards one or more customers.

Duties include the following:

- **Service delivery performance**: Responsible for the performance of the service toward assigned customers including all delivery activities.

- **Service delivery reporting**: Responsible for the delivery of performance reports to the customer as specified in the service level agreement.

- **Escalation management**: Responsible for reporting to management on all customer or delivery issues impacting the performance of the service. The delivery manager is also responsible for the resolution of all escalations and issues received from the different teams/units including customers.

- **Contract management**: Monitoring contract fulfilment from the customer and external service providers perspectives, including change request management.

- **Interface and process management**: Ensuring adherence to all processes required to deliver the service as contracted and that all internal functions, suppliers, and partner interfaces are operating as required.

- **Service Level Management**: Responsible for adherence to the T&C set out in the service level agreement.

- **Requirements management**: Responsible for receiving and filtering customer requirements monitoring progress until the requests are completed.

DevOps

The DevOps organization consists of senior engineers and solution architects responsible for providing the interface between R&D, operations teams, and other technical organizations. The DevOps organization is responsible for specific customer implementations (including customizations) and the lifecycle management of the service from a technical perspective.

Duties include the following:

- Technical ownership of all customer-deployed services

- Second-level support to resolve trouble tickets escalated from first-level support

- Evaluating and implementing lifecycle management and customizations

- Rapid feature deployment including prototyping for customers

- Requirements management support to classify and estimate the effort and activities required to implement new features

Engineering

The engineering function manages the current installed base of the service, including the software and hardware components. This organization is responsible for support, maintenance, and lifecycle management of the following components

- Local server hosting the ITS software and storage

- Onboard vehicle devices, including the driver console and point-of-sale devices

- Configuration management of released software

Service Desk

The Intelligent Transport Services service desk is implemented by the operations center. This organization acts as the primary interface for customers and stakeholders with queries and issues related to contracted services.

The service desk is the central coordinating function responsible for registering trouble tickets, service requests, work orders, and incidents that impact the performance of the service.

Requests can be received via the following:

- Telephone

- E-mail

- Web forum

The service desk may answer the query or forward to the appropriate supporting function using the details specified in the procedures manual.

If a trouble ticket is required, it will be recorded in the trouble ticket system and forwarded to the appropriate organization for investigation and resolution.

This function will monitor the activity flow of all requests through the trouble ticketing system.

Service Delivery Functions

The service delivery functions required to implement and operate the ITS service are executed by the service delivery organization. They consist of the following:

- ITS Service management

- ITS Service assurance

- ITS Demand management

ITS Service Management

Service management functions are under the responsibility of the (regional and customer-specific) delivery managers. These managers monitor operational activities to ensure SLA compliance and efficient management of resources from the service delivery and operational organizations. They are responsible for the following functions.

Service delivery management: Service delivery management is responsible for the management of all customer-related delivery and operational issues including the performance reporting. The performance is measured against the KPIs and the service levels specified in the customer service level agreement. All escalations and relevant issues are managed by this function and reported monthly.

Requirements management and customization requests are managed by the delivery management providing assessment of requests and monitoring of progress until completion.

Contract management: Contract management is the responsibility of the delivery managers where contractual deviations are managed via the contract change request procedure. Non-compliance of the contract from either the customer or the delivery organization are handled through escalations and should be reviewed in the monthly performance review meeting.

Interface and process managment: The interface and process management function ensures that all necessary interfaces between internal and external organizations are operational and performing as defined in this document and the procedures manual.

Service level management: Adherence to all agreements (WLAs and SLAs) signed as part of the Intelligent Transport Service will be managed by this function. Deviations should be managed as escalations between the signatories of the agreement.

Fraud: All registered fraud incidents should be investigated by the DevOps organization and will be managed by the delivery manager. By default, fraud issues are given maximum priority until proven otherwise.

ITS Service Assurance

Service assurance falls under the responsibility of the service manager and is implemented by the operations center, DevOps, and R&D functions. It is responsible for service monitoring and performing corrective actions to ensure the service is performing according to the SLA. It is measured by the availability of the services and the KPIs defined in the Service Level Agreement.

Service assurance of the Intelligent Transport Service includes the following functions:

- Service desk functions (as described previously)
- First-level assurance services
- Second-level assurance services

Figure C-5 illustrates the management flow of trouble tickets and issues affecting the service performance. Each function managing the trouble ticket should attempt resolve the issue if possible. If they are unable to resolve the issue, it should be classified and allocated to the appropriate organization in the next level of support.

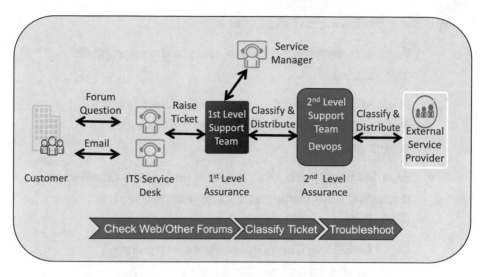

Figure C-5. *Operations assurance flow*

Note   The allocation of activities to be performed by first- or second-level support depends on the complexity and on the competence available at each level. There may be a need for third-level support that is provided by R&D.

First-Level Assurance

The following activities are the responsibility of the first-level support team. Performance will be measured by ticket volumes received in compliance with the SLA.

Note   The dimensioning of the organization should reflect the number of forecasted tickets. If this value is exceeded, it can result in reduced performance without penalization.

Specific activities include the following:

- **Fault management**: Escalate issues to the appropriate organization.

- **Fault coordination**: Act as a central point to receive and distribute information between operational organizations.

- **First-level support**: Analyze issues and events detected through external sources or alarms and attempt resolution.

- **Event handling**: Classify cases/events and assign problem categories and status codes.

- **Security incident response**: Escalate security issues to the appropriate support organization.

- **Control and support reactive of planned activities**: Support field maintenance with assistance as required.

- **Management notification and escalation**: Act as a central information source for all escalations to ITS service management and stakeholders. Provide regular updates on the progress according to the service level classification.

- **First-level routine maintenance**: Perform remote scheduled routine maintenance activities as defined by DevOps. Support the day-to-day running of the ITS systems such as log file storage, files transfer, and so on.

- **Site control**: Maintain a log of personnel that are on the premises or remotely connected to the service.

Second-Level Assurance

The following activities are the responsibility of the second delivery support team and the DevOps organization. The performance of this function will be measured by ticket volumes received and compliance to the SLA.

Note   The dimensioning of the organization should reflect the number of forecasted tickets. If this value is exceeded, it can result in reduced performance.

Specific activities include the following:

- **Second-level support**: Perform fault analysis and corrective actions to restore the service.

- **Fault coordination**: Interface between contributing support organizations as defined in WLAs and SLAs to rectify faults as required.

- **System administration**: Perform regular corrective and conditioning tasks on system components to adhere to the defined service levels.

- **Database administration**: Perform regular corrective and conditioning tasks on all databases to ensure they perform as required.

- **Application administration**: Perform regular corrective and conditioning tasks on all applications and services to ensure the applications and services perform within the defined service levels.

- **Back up and restore administration**: Perform regular corrective and conditioning tasks on the storage area and manage the backup schedule.

- **Technical impact analysis of proposed change requests**: Perform impact analysis to ensure that changes will not have unexpected impacts on customer service or security and ensure that the change implementation procedures are followed correctly.

- **Routine schedule definition and coordination**: Establish and maintain the schedule of routine activities to be performed to maintain service performance as required.

- **Second-level routine maintenance**: Perform scheduled remote maintenance tasks such as manually testing system performance, performing backups, analyzing faults records and system logs.

- **Security incident investigations**: Conduct and support investigations triggered by security incidents.

- **Security control**: Maintain all agreed security logging functions in the system.

- **Deployment of system updates and upgrades**: Update/upgrade service elements with new software and configurations as required.

ITS Demand Management

Demand Management falls under the responsibility of the service manager and is implemented by the operations center (containing the fulfilment organisation) and DevOps. This function handles customer service requests, in other words, requests that are not fault related such as deployment of devices in newly commissioned vehicles.

Note   The customer is the client contracting the service, not the end customer using ITS.

The handling of requests is illustrated by Figure C-6. Requests are received by the service desk to be analyzed and classified. Requests can be received by e-mail or by entering questions in a customer forum that is being monitored by the ITS service desk. New service requirement requests will be sent to the Delivery manager and will be handled in the requirements process. Requests that fall within the scope of the service (as defined in the service description) will be allocated to the appropriate organization.

Each request will be managed according to the performance KPIs outlined in service level agreement.

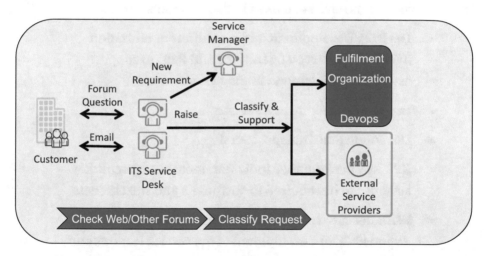

Figure C-6. *Demand management flow*

Specific activities include the following:

- Capacity expansions to the existing service, for example, deployment of onboard transport devices to enable fleet expansion

- Service modifications that fall within the service scope and do not require customizations, in other words, configuration settings

247

- System integration requests can be accepted for third-party products not included in the current service

- Report generation outside the scope outlined in the service description or specific reports requested on demand

Definitions, Acronyms, and Abbreviations

The following terms have been used in this appendix:

- **DevOps**: Development and operations organization interfacing between operations and R&D to support assurance and demand management

- **IaaS**: Infrastructure as a service

- **ITS**: Intelligent Transport Service

- **KPI**: Key performance indicator; measures specific key activities to be reported to customers and stakeholders

- **R&D**: Research and development organization responsible for development of the service features and expert assurance support

- **PaaS**: Platform as a service

- **P&L**: Profit and loss

- **SaaS**: Software as a service

- **SD&O**: Service delivery and operations; the organization responsible for the delivery and operational activities as defined in the service description

- **Service Request**: A request from the customer falling within the scope of the service

- **SLA**: Service level agreement; the contract signed between and external organizations

- **T&C**: Terms and conditions

- **Trouble Ticket**: An issue reported as a possible fault

- **WLA**: Work level agreement; the contract signed between internal service owner organizations, defining the level of service agreed between both parties

APPENDIX D

Responsibility Matrix

This appendix illustrates the Intelligent Transport Service responsibility matrix (see Table D-1). The matrix defines the roles and responsibilities for each organization contributing to the service.

Definitions

R:	Responsible	The assigned person is responsible for executing the action (or actions) to complete an activity.
A:	Accountable	The assigned person is accountable for the completion of the activity.
S:	Support	The assigned person provides support for executing the tasks required to complete the activity.
C:	Consult	The assigned person is consulted on key issues and decisions that occur while executing tasks for the assigned activity.
I:	Informed	The assigned person is regularly updated on the progress of the tasks being executed to complete an activity.
A/R:	Accountable/ Responsible	The assigned person is accountable and will perform the activities required to complete the activity.

Note: The person (or organization) accountable for an activity may delegate the responsibility to another person (or organization). They remain accountable for its successful execution although they do not carry out the execution.

© Barry Haughian 2018
B. Haughian, *Design, Launch, and Scale IoT Services*,
https://doi.org/10.1007/978-1-4842-3712-0

Note   Table D-1 is for illustration purposes only; many of the roles can be combined into one role in smaller organizations.

Table D-1. *Responsibility Matrix*

Intelligent Transport Service Responsibility Matrix

	Legend
R	Responsible
A	Accountable
S	Support
C	Consult
I	Inform

Category	Process	Service Management	Business Owner	Local Service Manager	Operations Centre	ITS Service Desk	Reporting Unit	1st Level Assurance	2nd Level Assurance	Order Management	Incident Manager	Coordination Manager	Problem Manager	Process Driver	Change Manager	Asset Management	Security Manager	Service Delivery & Operations	Head of Operations	Assurance Manager	Deployment Manager	Service Delivery Manager	Service Desk	Service Desk Support	Field Operations	Device Support	Research & Development	R&D Team	Devops	Devops Engineering Team
Request Fulfilment	Onboard Device Deployment									R		C		R						A	S	R			R					
	Deployment of Gateway	S	S		S		S	I	R					R					I	I	I									
Service Reporting	Service Delivery Performance				R						I									A		S			R		S			
	Real-time Reporting																													A/R
Fault Management	Incident Management	R			R		R	S		R										A								R		R
	Investigation and Diagnostics	R			R		R	R		A												R						R		R
	Resolution and Recovery	R			R		R	R		A	I	I								R		R			R			R		R
	Reporting	S			S		S	S		S	I	R								S	A		S					R		R
Event Management	Active Monitoring Execution	I			A/R		R																							
	Infrastructure Monitoring	R			R		R	S		A									I		I		I							
Field Operations Process	Management of Cameras							S	S											A		S		S	R					
	Management of Gateways							S	S											A	SS			S	R					
	Work Order Management									R						I				A					R	S				
	Inventory Management																A								R	A/R				
Access Management	Control Users Access Rights	R			R		R	R									S	A/R												
	Monitor Access Management	R			R		R										S	A/R					S		S					
Service Transition	Change Management (Process)							S	S		R		R	R				A/R		S	S									
	Release Approval	I			I		I	I	I	I	I	I		R											I			S		S
	Maintain Asset plan																A/R		I	I	I	I		S			R	I		I
	Monitor Performance										I						A/R		I	I	I	I			R			I		I
	Requirements Handling										I					A				S				R		C		S		S
Contract Management	Global WLA Fulfillment										R							A/R												
	Requirements Handling										I			I				A/R	I	I	I									

252

Table D-1. (*continued*)

Intelligent Transport Service Responsibility Matrix		
R	Responsible	
A	Accountable	
S	Support	
C	Consult	
I	Inform	

Column headers (rotated): Service Management · Business Owner · Local Service Manager · Operations Centre · ITS Service Desk · Reporting Unit · 1st Level Assurance · 2nd Level Assurance · Order Management · Incident Manager · Coordination Manager · Problem Manager · Process Driver · Change Manager · Asset Management · Security Manager · Service Delivery & Operations · Head of Operations · Assurance Manager · Deployment Manager' · Service Delivery Manager · Service Desk · Service Desk Support · Field Operations · Device Support · Research & Development · R&D Team · Devops · Devops Engineering Team

Role	Description
Service Management	
Business Owner	Responsible for Profit and Loss on the Service
Local Service Manager	Responsible for the Delivery towards a specific customer and intefacing to the Account owner
Operations Centre	
ITS Service Desk	Central SPOC(Single Point of Contact) receving and distributing requests received by Operations centre
Reporting Unit	Responsible for the production of all reports
1st Level Assurance	Basic Troubleshooting
2nd Level Assurance	Advanced Troubleshooting
Order Management	Execution Service Requests
Incident Manager	Managing Emergencies and escalations
Coordination Manager	Interfacing with Service Management
Problem Manager	Follow-up Management of Emergencies
Process Driver	Responsible for process efficiency and adherence
Change Manager	Responsible for adherence to Change control process
Asset Management	Management of ITS devices and Service assets
Security Manager	Security Manager
Service Delivery & Operations	
Head of Operations	Responsible for Delivery and Operations
Assurance Manager	Responsible for KPI Assurance Adherence
Deployment Manager'	Responsible for Service Request execution
Service Delivery Manager	Service Delivery Manager
Service Desk	
Service Desk Support	Central coordinating function for customer requests and issues
Field Operations	
Device Support	Responsible for all field Operations activities for deployed devices
Research & Development	
Service Desk Support	Central coordinating function for customer requests and issues
Devops	
Device Support	Responsible for all field Operations activities for deployed devices

Glossary

This glossary explains the abbreviations and terminology used throughout the book.

- **AaS**: As a service; a business model where the customer is charged according to usage volumes.

- **AI**: Artificial intelligence; algorithms and techniques implemented to create intelligent automatically adapting functions.

- **API**: Application Programming Interface; a set of functions and procedures that allow the creation of applications that access the features or data of an operating system, application, or other service. In most scenarios, defines the interaction between the application layer and the platform layer.

- **B2B**: Business to business.

- **B2BGW**: Business-to-business gateway; offers the ability to connect external services with the purpose of transferring data securely.

- **CRM**: Customer relationship management; a suite of tools that support the management of customers for the service organizations.

- **DevOps**: A Development and Operations organization consisting of engineers providing service development and operational competence.

© Barry Haughian 2018
B. Haughian, *Design, Launch, and Scale IoT Services*,
https://doi.org/10.1007/978-1-4842-3712-0

- **Ecosystem (IoT)**: A collection of collaborators, companies, and individuals cooperating in the development of IoT services.

- **ESB**: Enterprise service bus. Software that facilitates the communication and coordination between components in the IoT stack

- **FIWARE**: Supported by the Future Internet Public-Private Partnership (FI-PPP).

- **GDPR**: General Data Protection Regulation, the regulations introduced by the European Union, aimed at protecting user data.

- **GTM**: Go to market; the strategy employed describing how to sell a service commercially.

- **GUI**: Graphical user interface; the software interface used to access a service.

- **Hybrid cloud**: An integrated cloud service utilizing both private and public clouds.

- **IaaS**: Infrastructure as a service; a cloud service offering infrastructure components (such as virtual machines) in an as-a-service model.

- **IDE**: Integrated development environment; a suite of tools facilitating the development of software.

- **IMSI**: International Mobile Subscriber Identity; used to identify the user of a cellular network.

- **Industry 4.0**: Creates a "smart factory" with the modular implementation of cyber-physical systems, monitoring physical processes, automation, and data exchange in manufacturing technologies and processes.

- **IoT**: Internet of Things.

- **IoT ecosystem**: The contributors that enable IoT services to be implemented and evolve.

- **IPR**: Intellectual property rights.

- **ISO270001**: An information security standard published by the International Organization for Standardization (ISO).

- **ITIL**: Information Technology Infrastructure Library; a suite of practices and methodologies designed to deliver IT services.

- **ITS**: Intelligent Transport Service.

- **KPI**: Key performance indicator; the most important measurements being recorded used to evaluate the service performance.

- **Managed services**: A managed services provider in IoT assumes responsibility for providing a defined set of services to ensure the service meets SLA obligations, usually via a managed operations agreement.

- **M2M**: Machine to machine; the communication between two devices.

- **Multidomestic**: Service provided by GMA that allows localization of SIMs.

- **NDA**: Nondisclosure agreement.

- **NOC**: Network operations center; an organization that monitors an IoT service.

- **NB – IoT**: Narrow Band – IoT; a radio technology.

- **Number portability**: Enables mobile telephone users to retain their mobile telephone numbers when changing from one mobile network carrier to another.

- **Opex**: Operational expenditure; the costs incurred to operate the business.

- **OSI**: Open Systems Interconnection; a model defining the internal structure of an IT service.

- **PaaS**: Platform as a service; a cloud service offering platform-layer components permitting the development and management of applications and services.

- **P&L**: Profit and loss.

- **PLC**: Power line communication; a communication method that uses electrical wiring to simultaneously carry data and electric power.

- **POC**: Proof of concept; a service that can exhibit the functionality but cannot be delivered commercially.

- **Public cloud**: A cloud service in which a service provider makes resources, such as applications and storage, available to the general public over the Internet.

- **Private cloud**: A distinct and secure cloud-based environment in which only the specified client can operate.

- **QOS**: Quality of service.

- **R&D**: Research and development; an organization responsible for the development of the service.

- **RASCI**: A matrix defining the service organizations and their roles in the delivery of activities (Responsibilities, Accountabilities, Support, Consultative, and Informed).

- **SaaS**: Software as a service; offers software in a licensed subscription basis.

- **SDK**: Service development kit; the software development tools that allow the creation of applications.

- **SD&O**: Service delivery and operations; the organization responsible for delivering and operating the service commercially.

- **Service desk**: Organization that acts as the central coordinating function for the service.

- **Service request**: Request from a customer that requires a modification of the existing service.

- **SIM-OTA**: SIM over-the-air; a technology used to communicate with, download applications to, and manage a SIM card without being connected physically to the card

- **SLA**: Service level agreement; the contract signed between the service organization and the external service provider defining the service levels contracted.

- **SOC 1**: Service Organization Controls 1 report; a report on controls at a service organization that are relevant to user entities' internal control over financial reporting.

- **SOC 2**: Service Organization Controls 2 report; a report that confirms the service provider has the best internal practices in place to verify the security, availability, and privacy in your data hosting environment.

- **SSAE 16**: Statement on Standards for Attestation Engagements 16; an auditing standard for service organizations.

- **T&C**: Terms and conditions.

- **3PP**: Third-party provider; an external organization providing a product or service.

- **Tier 1**: A large company with a global reach and an R&D organization.

- **Tier 2**: A small or medium company with little or no R&D.

- **Tier 3**: A small company with no R&D and supplying locally.

- **Trouble ticket**: An issue reported as a possible fault.

- **UI**: User interface.

- **UI framework**: User interface framework; a software suite that presents the user with APIs so that they can build their own UI components or modify the UI itself.

- **Vertical market**: A market in which vendors offer goods and services specific to an industry, trade, profession, or other group of customers with specialized requirements

- **Virtual SIM**: Provides remote SIM provisioning and GSM connectivity without the need for having a physical SIM in the device.

- **VPN**: Virtual private network; extends a private network across a public network enabling users to send and receive data across shared or public networks.

- **Watson**: A cloud application tool that includes analytics services providing big data processing.

- **WLA**: Work level agreement; a contract signed between internal service organizations outlining ways of working and delivery levels.

- **XaaS**: Any service delivered in an as-a-service business model.

References

Table 1. *Contains an explanation of the abbreviations and terminology used throughout the book*

Ref. 1 (Ch. 1)	IoT Trend Watch 2017 IHS Markit `https://ihsmarkit.com/index.html`
Ref. 2 (Ch. 1)	IoT Devices to Outnumber Humans in 2017 by Michael Alba `www.engineering.com`
Ref. 3 (Ch. 3)	5 Keys to Designing Great UX for IoT Products IoT For All `www.iotforall.com`
Ref. 4 (Ch. 3)	The Developer's Guide to IoT IoT Agenda `https://internetofthingsagenda.techtarget.com`

Ref. 5 (Ch. 3)	IoT Security Foundation, Best Practice Guidelines
	`https://www.iotsecurityfoundation.org/`
	`best-practice-guidelines`

Ref. 6 (Ch. 3)	Data Sharing, Advanced Analytics, and Success with IoT MIT Sloan Review `https://sloanreview.mit.edu`
Ref. 7 (Ch. 3)	Smart Cows and How Not to Design IoT Products to Fail by Cheryl Ailuni RFID Journal `http://www.rfidjournal.com/internet-of-things`

(continued)

© Barry Haughian 2018
B. Haughian, *Design, Launch, and Scale IoT Services,*
https://doi.org/10.1007/978-1-4842-3712-0

Table 1. (*continued*)

Ref. 8 (Ch. 3)	Keeping Cybersecurity Spending on Track as IoT Adoption Swells Internet of Things Institute `http://www.ioti.com` (`www.iotworldtoday.com`)
Ref. 9 (Ch. 3)	Overcome IoT Security Challenges IoT Agenda `https://internetofthingsagenda.techtarget.com/`
Ref. 10 (Ch. 5)	IoT: Harnessing Device Data `http://www.dzone.com`
Ref. 11 (Ch. 6)	Internet Geeks `https://www.internetgeeks.org`
Ref. 12 (Ch. 6)	Internet of Things Council Eco-system `https://www.theinternetofthings.eu/`
Ref. 13 (Ch. 6)	IEEE Internet of Things `iot.ieee.org`
Ref. 14 (Ch. 7)	Comparing Platforms to Add Internet of Things Capabilities to Products `www.engineering.com`
Ref. 15 (Ch. 8)	Forecasts Worldwide Spending on the Internet of Things to Reach $772 Billion in 2018 IDC `https://www.idc.com`
Ref. 16 (Ch. 8)	IoT Business News `https://iotbusinessnews.com`
Ref. 17 (Ch. 8)	RFID Journal `http://www.rfidjournal.com/internet-of-things`

(*continued*)

Table 1. (*continued*)

Ref. 18 (Ch. 8)	IoT and analytics market for utilities expected to grow to $5.1bn in 2028 IoT News `https://www.iottechnews.com`
Ref. 19 (Ch. 8)	"IoTone Accelerating the Industrial Internet of Things" `www.iotone.com`
Ref. 20 (Ch. 10)	10 Questions to Ask an IoT Platform Provider `www.engineering.com`
Ref. 21 (Ch. 10)	80 percent of organisations set to invest in AI `https://internetofbusiness.com`

Index

© Barry Haughian 2018
B. Haughian, *Design, Launch, and Scale IoT Services*,
https://doi.org/10.1007/978-1-4842-3712-0